"If you are satisfied with the 'sa[me] choice of Bible study books, put this book down and return to your regularly scheduled stuff. If, however, you would like a fresh trip through truth from someone who talks with you instead of at you, get a copy for yourself, one for each of your best girlfriends, and make a standing appointment to ingest dangerous carbs and share what you learn in these pages."

—ANITA RENFROE, comedian; musician; author of *The Purse-Driven Life* and *A Purse-Driven Christmas*

"Jen Hatmaker writes a creative, funny, down-to-earth book that will encourage and equip women (and even a few curious men) to read and actually understand their Bibles. This fresh study will change your life as you cry, 'Word of God, speak.'"

—ED YOUNG, senior pastor, Fellowship Church; author of *You! The Journey to the Center of Your Worth*

"Stick close to Jen Hatmaker and you'll soon be skydiving into God's Word in a not-for-sissies faith adventure. Her passion for knowing God is contagious and wonderful!"

—VIRELLE KIDDER, conference speaker; author of *Donkeys Still Talk*

A Modern Girl's Guide to Bible Study

A Refreshingly Unique Look at God's Word

JEN HATMAKER

NAVPRESS

A NavPress resource published in alliance
with Tyndale House Publishers, Inc.

NAVPRESS●

NavPress is the publishing ministry of The Navigators, an international Christian organization and leader in personal spiritual development. NavPress is committed to helping people grow spiritually and enjoy lives of meaning and hope through personal and group resources that are biblically rooted, culturally relevant, and highly practical.

For more information, visit www.NavPress.com.

Contents

* * * *Preface* * * *

Welcome! I already feel as if I know you. We're that generation who raise our kids while running businesses and keeping the church afloat. (You know we do.) And, as for me, I feel more like a "girl" than anything else. Girls snort when they laugh, and they sometimes watch reality TV. My mom and her friends are "women."

I've prayed and prayed for this moment for you: a new beginning. I hope by the end of this trip you will have learned, been freed, grown, gained confidence, laughed out loud (because I'm a bit off), fallen in love with Scripture, and been changed forever.

Just a quick note: If you will be using the study guide with a small group, partner, or on your own, turn to it first before you begin reading. It paces your reading out over the course of five weeks. If you're the lucky girl who got roped into leading a small group, there's a leader's guide back there, too.

This is for us Modern Girls. I won't call you "beloved." I don't use phrases like *flying on the tender wings of angels*. I might have even used words like *boobs* or *loopholes to submission* (both of which have problems). But I do love God's Word desperately, and I pray that you will, too. Let's link arms like modern girlfriends do and walk together.

* * * *Acknowledgments* * * *

For my Favorite God: Thank You for using a silly girl to champion Your Word. I love You so dearly. My heart overflows with a good theme.

To my Girlfriends, my special companions on this journey. Thank you for teaching me, laughing at me, cheering me on, ingesting Benadryl at Christi's every Thursday, loving the Word, driving with me (and sending me) to New Mexico, editing without cutting my favorite stories, test-driving all this material when you didn't have time, enduring my self-absorption, and allowing me to flaunt your lives in print. As my mom always tells me, "You have exceptional friends. Don't run them off." I love you as much as any girl has ever loved her friends. You know I do.

Thank you, husband of mine. You've been a believer since the beginning when I was a swirling vortex of uncertainty. That mattered so much. And thanks for genetically endowing our three kids with much insanity, as they will be an endless source of material for both of us. (I suppose we collaborated on the DNA buffet: You gave them impossible cowlicks and OCD tendencies; I gave them a propensity for drama and road rage.) I love you forever.

I am so grateful to my Lake Hills Church family. You have been my safe place to learn, to sprout wings, to crash and burn, and to grow. For your patience, support, unconditional love, and countless opportunities for me to make or break your various events, I love and thank you.

And thanks to Rachelle Gardner, who set this thing in motion based on an "instant connection" that was neither proven nor safe. I'm clearly high risk. To Karen Lee-Thorp, Terry Behimer, and my new friends at NavPress: It's a true pleasure to work with the varsity team. This JV writer thanks you for a fabulous initiation.

Part One

I'm Less Intimidated Reading Shape Magazine

Common Insecurities About Studying God's Word

I've never cared to spend large quantities of time with people smarter than me. It's so annoying. I have enough problems to worry about without trying to manage adult academic peer pressure. I mean, really. Life is too short for that kind of stress.

The last thing I need is for the intellectuals to pat my cute, simple head while making mental notes to spend more time with me, hoping I might soak up a fraction of their scholarly aura. You know the ones—they have the word-of-the-day flip cards on their desks so they can drop impressive vocabulary such as *parturient*. I'd rather play Barbie Rapunzel with my daughter because, quite frankly, there is a possibility I am smarter than she is, although the verdict is still out on that one. (Don't ask her.)

Let's not even talk about spending time with people more spiritual than me. I've got enough on my plate trying to sound smarter. I can't lace that with wisdom and Scripture and godliness, too. I get dizzy, and my throat starts constricting. That can't be normal.

Have you ever listened to a More Spiritual Friend talk about the complexity of her relationship with God? While she explains how she hears His voice every time the wind blows through the trees and a new flower blooms in her garden, have you hoped He doesn't tell her how you went on a psychotic rampage that morning when your two-year-old smashed an entire box of Lucky Charms into your living room carpet and you actually looked up the phone number for your local foster care rep? Me neither, of course, but I know people like that. It's sad, really.

If you're wondering if my average portion of the universal dispersion of giftedness bothers me, let me reassure you—it doesn't. Regularness suits me. I am not an academic scholar or a spiritual giant, which I'm fine with because it probably means more people like me. It's hard to love the perfect ones; they make us look so bad. It's telling that I have many good friends.

I am flawed on many obvious levels, and truthfully, I erroneously report my zip code at least two out of every ten times. So why would I write about pursuing a rich understanding of the Bible? Isn't that material reserved for the upper echelon of the church hierarchy? The ones who have "arrived"?

The answer is fundamental: The insights of the Bible are not reserved for pastors, their wives, and Billy Graham. Psalm 119:130, one of the most beautiful passages concerning God's Word, says,

The unfolding of Your words gives light;
It gives understanding to the *simple*.

Well, my stars—that's me. Maybe it's you, too. There's just
the matter of unfolding what's in there. The Bible is tightly
packed sometimes, isn't it?

I recently spent an entire day doing laundry. The "entire
day" part should tell you we were all wearing our last pair
of clean underwear. There had been a sustained neglect of
domestic duties, which, apparently, I'm in charge of. My bed
was filled with neatly folded piles of clothes. All the stacks
were straight and arranged by subcategories (I have a lot of
issues).

I brought the last load into my bedroom to fold, although
I certainly wasn't planning on putting them away for at least
another day, which is a charming habit my husband adores.
But instead, I found my three kids on the bed jumping on,
hiding under, and tossing up every piece of clothing I'd spent
all day folding.

While I was trying to remember where I put that foster
care number, I yelled, "What possessed your three little minds
to mess up everything I just folded?" My oldest son, Gavin,
looked at me as if I sometimes don't understand this life at
all and said, "It was fun." (My daughter—with leggings and
underwear draped on her head—answered, "I didn't do it,"
but sometimes she lies, and that's a different book on parenting and/or anxiety management.) Unfolding was fun.

Indeed.

The last word most of us would use to describe Bible
study is *fun*. Unfolding Scripture is at best intimidating and
at worst drudgery. Now, *I* wanted my stacks to remain folded

until they magically transferred themselves into drawers, but my kids discovered the sheer joy of the unfolding process. They also discovered maternal domestic wrath, but they can work that out with their therapists later. God's desire is for us to encounter His Word truth by truth until there isn't a folded piece left. He wants to find us covered in Scripture and loving every minute of it.

God never intended for His Word to be a tidy, hands-off package with crisp edges and a wealth of mysteries that we set aside until Sunday morning. Unlike me, He's hollering at us, "Get in there! Turn My Word upside down and inside out. It's all for *you*." Or, even better (and possibly more accurate),

> "I am the LORD,
>   and there is no other.
> I have not spoken in secret,
>   from somewhere in a land of darkness;
> I have not said to Jacob's descendants,
>   'Seek me in vain.'
> I, the LORD, speak the truth;
>   I declare what is right." (Isaiah 45:18-19, NIV)

But there lies a great chasm between God's intentions and the way most of us feel about Bible study. I liken it to how I feel about running, which is best described as a long-distance love affair. Runners are so intriguing. They banter back and forth, "I have to run every morning, or my mind stays cloudy all day." I thought murkiness was normal, but I nod as though clarity is something I, too, achieve on a daily basis. They gush about their feet hitting the pavement ("It's so therapeutic!") and their lungs filling up with fresh air. I wonder why when I run, I resemble a cat with arthritis and my lungs feel less "filled with fresh air" and more "searing flames exploding through my chest cavity."

My Runner Friend Shelley tells me, "I'm sorry I'm grouchy today. I haven't run." On my off days, I say, "I'm sorry I'm grouchy today. I just am, so try very hard not to annoy or bother me in any way." What is it with these people? What do they know that I don't? How can they love this activity that is sheer punishment to me? I toss my head and blather, "You people are crazy! Run your slim little legs off. I'll be watching *Seinfeld* reruns."

Truthfully, I'd love to be a runner. I want to join their secret society and learn their fancy lingo and wear their special shoes. My Runner Friend Leslie says I have to do it more than twice a year. My other Runner Friend Stephanie asks me if I'm doing "interval running." You know what? Save the fancy talk for the other Club Members. I'm just trying to get some oxygen to my brain.

But I get it: My methods—or lack thereof—are hindering my progress. The runners lie and say anyone can do it if she learns a few guidelines and develops the habit. They urge me to come to their side and promise me I'll love it over there. I say, "Thank you for your kind input. I'll put that information in the 'I'll Really Consider This' file" (which is a misnomer for the "As If" file).

But this is how many believers perceive authentic Bible study. Sure, it's great for those who have the mystery figured out. We marvel at others who love God's Word and spend hours in it, only to emerge with insights that have never darkened the corners of our minds. We notice that Bible study causes them to ooze clarity and fulfillment, and we watch as they come alive through Scripture.

What is it with these people? Why does God speak to them through Scripture, but all we come out with are more questions and a migraine? Thousands of us dug our heels in at one point and proclaimed, "Attention! I am going to read the Bible this year from start to finish," only to get hopelessly sidetracked in Leviticus between the laws about sacrifices to the goat demons and the 57,400 sons of Zebulun. So we throw our hands up and put personal Bible study in the "I'll Really Consider This" file, knowing it will inevitably gather dust and become permanently shelved.

Chicks with Codependency Issues

So what seems to be the problem here? For most of us, it's simple. We've never learned how to study the Bible. We have two approaches: poor or none. We assume that reading the Bible equals studying the Bible, and we spiral down in frustration when it doesn't work.

It's like my kids' first trip to the dentist (three years late) when she pulled out floss and asked if they used it at morning or night. They said, "What's that?" and thereby firmly secured my place on the Dentists' List of Bad People. It was definitely something they needed to know, but they had never been taught because sometimes we're just trying to make sure everyone has on underwear and two of the same shoes, and we can't be worrying about dental floss.

Likewise, many of us have been believers for years but have never been taught how to study God's Word on our own. Most of the formats we encounter the Bible through are created or presented by someone else. An assumption emerges that the deep waters of the Bible can be explored only by the "enlightened," so what do we do? We become totally dependent on them to teach us God's Word.

How many of us have survived spiritually from Sunday morning to Sunday morning or from packaged Bible study to packaged Bible study with caverns in between? We pace and wring our hands in the gaps, and we mourn our fill-in-the-blanks and leading questions. We ask, "What am I supposed to read? When is the sign-up for the next study?" We allow the mysterious to remain folded until hopefully someone will tell us what it all means.

Now, before you yank out your laptops to send me scathing e-mails about the biblical principles of sound teaching, hear me out. The Bible is indeed clear about the designation of teachers uniquely gifted to build up the church. In 1 Corinthians 12:28, Paul writes, "And God has *appointed* in the church, first apostles, second prophets, third *teachers*, then miracles, then gifts of healings, helps, administrations, various kinds of tongues." Teachers are placed by the will of God for the common good.

I am not proposing that we collectively hold our hands up to our teachers and declare, "I'm done with you! Apparently I can figure this thing out on my own. Be gone with your knowledge and wisdom." Mercy, no. Jesus was our prime example as the Ultimate Teacher. He told His students in John 13:13, "You call Me *Teacher* and Lord; and you are right, for so I am." Where would our dearest disciples have been without their Teacher? Still schlepping fish and dozing off in the tax-collector booth, no doubt.

Likewise, packaged Bible studies we buy at the Christian bookstore or work through in a small group are powerful and create new layers in our spiritual growth. These are wonderful places to learn how to navigate the Bible and become exposed to God. My Bible Study Friend Christina says this is where she had her hand held in Scripture until she was ready to walk on her own.

God has given teachers experiences and wisdom they obediently steward. They lead us down paths they've journeyed and create opportunities for new paths to be cleared in our lives. Bravo! I stand up and applaud them. I whistle. I blow kisses. We should always be learning from our teachers because that is God's design. Don't drop out of your Bible study group or stage a book burning on the front lawn of your church. Books and Bible studies will forever be tools by which we are stretched spiritually.

But what about when they're over?

As My Son Used to Say, "I'm Afeared!"

For many of us, the problem with personal Bible study is rooted in fear. Trying something we have no skill at is intimidating and overwhelming—like the day I brought my first-born home and realized I was supposed to be a parent. What? Who thought I could do this? Does anyone know for sure that I qualify to manage another human? And why won't this baby stop crying?

In the Word, we're often plagued by the sheer weight of the unknown before we encounter step one. Fear manifests itself in many ways: fear of lacking knowledge, fear of failure, fear of weird Bible lingo (what's with "propitiation"?), fear of that fine print on the sides and bottom of the pages.

There's also a fear of clipping along at a decent pace only

to get tripped up by something confusing. What on earth do I do then? Can I plug my pastor's cell phone number into speed dial? Do these intrusions annoy him? This often becomes "a good stopping place," never to be voyaged through again.

As my Bible Study Friend Erin pointed out, there also lurks the fear of being changed. It's safer to secure salvation and then simply coast in complacency. Even at a fundamental level, most believers realize that God's Word is a powerful place, and no one who enters will emerge the same. What if the Bible requires more than we want to give — or give up?

My Bible Study Friend Amy voiced her fear of commitment. Digging into Scripture doesn't have the feel of a three-minute-a-day effort. In her sixteen-hour day, she averages forty-two minutes of unaccounted time. She can squeak out forty-five if she hits green lights. How is real Bible study going to fit into real life? It would be a luxury to sit down with God's Word for as long as we need, pouring undistracted energy into understanding Scripture, but this is a reality for exactly . . . no one I know.

One thing is sure: These are not just the concerns of new believers. My Girlfriend Trina found Christ as an adult, a situation that came with a built-in set of insecurities. The questions outnumbered the answers, and even worse, it appeared that everyone else already had it figured out. But I went to church three times a week as a fetus and gave my heart to Jesus when I was six, and I also spent years of unsuccessful time in the Word. Same fears, same insecurities. I never learned *how* to embrace the Bible; I just heard, "Read it." As a minister's kid, I assumed there was some genetic coding that hadn't kicked in. All I could figure was that I would just grow up one day and it would all be clear.

Wonderful modeling doesn't necessarily transfer either. My Bible Study Friend Christi grew up watching her mom fill volumes of journals while memorizing most of the Bible, yet that magic connection eluded her when she dug in. Why do we genetically receive the propensity for stretch marks, but we can't inherit what our moms understood about Scripture? On many levels, life is unfair.

I believe it is the conspicuous minority in our churches that are accomplished students of the Bible. It seems like "everyone" has it under control only because the ones in the spotlight are confident in the Word. In truth, most run-of-the-mill believers would admit that personal Bible study is a puzzle on one level or another. We'd love to get more from Scripture, but we don't know how to get it.

What about you?

What about in the quiet of your bedroom when it's just you and God? When the small group is over and it is early morning before the family wakes up. What do you do? You might ask the same questions I asked for years: What do I read? Where do I start? Where do I stop? What happens when I don't get it? Is this just face-value meaning, or is there more? How is this going to affect me? Did I turn the coffee on? (I often got distracted.)

Most of us bring insecurity to the table when we meet with God. We're not sure what to do with the Bible when it's all by itself without a workbook or a devotional or a teacher. We scratch our heads at the psalmist's words:

O how I love Your law!
It is my meditation all the day.
Your commandments make me wiser than my enemies,

For they are ever mine.
I have more insight than all my teachers,
For Your testimonies are my meditation.
I understand more than the aged,
Because I have observed Your precepts. (119:97-100)

What? Where is this confidence coming from? And what's with this "all the day" talk? I was lucky to hammer out ten minutes of reading and even luckier if I could remember four words of it by lunch. "More insight than all my teachers"? That's just crazy talk, isn't it?

In short: No.

Every woman who says "I believe" has the opportunity to fall in love with the Bible and understand its beautiful layers just as God intended. Let's learn to unfold the perfect stacks of truth God has set forth in His Word until we're covered in them.

And I promise it will be fun.

I have become its servant by the commission God gave me to present to you *the word of God in its fullness*—the mystery that has been kept hidden for ages and generations, but is now disclosed to the saints. To them *God has chosen to make known among the Gentiles* the glorious riches of this mystery. (Colossians 1:25-27, NIV)

* * * CHAPTER 2 * * *

Nair, Diet Pills, and Other Things That Don't Work

Ineffective Strategies for Connecting with Scripture

Our daughter, Sydney, is a free spirit, which is code for "visits us on earth occasionally and confuses us with her imaginings." She'll probably be a misunderstood artist. She is always dressed in some manner that is clearly not normal, but I choose sanity over wardrobe wrangling. Over time, I have built up an impressive immunity to the stares of strangers who wear khaki pants and matching shoes.

Sydney dwells under a spotlight only she can see and bursts into song whenever the urge seizes her. The amount of discretion exercised for these impromptu concerts is zero. She is all about her music. She can't help it if she becomes musically possessed in Target. Artists can't control when inspiration strikes.

Sydney's singing involves liberties that would bring much distress to the artistically gifted. For starters, she inserts extraneous words not intended to be there. Sydney might sing, "Jesus loves the little children, all the children of the world. But He loves me the most, and it's too bad that Caleb is such a bad boy who doesn't ever mind because now Jesus is probably mad at him"—all to music, of course.

But the real problem is in the execution. Her concerts involve piercing renditions that are vicious butcherings of the composers' intentions. The notes slur together in an off-key fashion, and the volume is loud enough to cause inner-ear damage in young children. All the while, she closes her eyes, sways her head around like Janis Joplin, and makes her rock-star face, which I've caught her practicing many, many times in her mirror.

It's painful.

My husband and I think this is hilarious, and we often ask her to sing in front of our friends to find out which ones will lie to us the most about her "music." It's a character test. None of them have passed. But when the performances have our ears ringing and our vision blurring, we holler out, "Baby! For the love of everything good and pure! What is coming out of your mouth?" With dramatic eye rolling, she clues us in: "Hello—I'm singing." Sure you are. Tell that to your voice coach someday.

In the same way, what we often define as Bible study is largely an exercise in futility with occasional moments of insight. If asked, we'd say, "Sure, I read the Bible. I love that thing." But the truth is, we approach God's Word without any strategies to make it come alive.

Sydney says she is singing, but she is actually mass-producing headaches. Many of us say we're studying the Bible, yet we're coming away empty-handed. This isn't because we're terrible people who spout lies and cheat on our taxes; it's just that most of us don't know any different. We haven't encountered the full strength of the Word, so we assume our reality is all there is. Truthfully, we are experiencing a lesser version of biblical possibilities.

Why do we get stuck there? Why don't we press on for more? For the same reason I hit that 4:30 p.m. breaking point and resort to locking my kids in the backyard with a tub of half-inflated basketballs and a box of Popsicles, hoping to survive one more hour until my husband comes home: We simply don't know what else to do.

When Bad Methods Happen to Good and Cute Girls

In those moments carved out for prayer and God's Word, I've come across (and by that I mean I've tried) many poor approaches to authentic Bible study, such as the old randomly-open-the-Bible-to-whatever-page-and-see-if-there-is-something-inspiring-there method: "God, wherever my finger lands, that must be Your word for me today." You know you've done it. So have I. We wonder why we can't find instant enlightenment in the second chapter of Nahum. After all, that's where the Bible fell open all by itself.

Believers, God crafted this world with exact precision down to the tiniest molecule of DNA, so why would He intend for the study of His Word to be random? When in His history has He ever functioned haphazardly? Jeremiah wrote,

Thus says the LORD,
Who gives the sun for light by day
And the fixed order of the moon and the stars
    for light by night,
Who stirs up the sea so that its waves roar;
The LORD of hosts is His name:
"If this *fixed order* departs
From before Me," declares the LORD,
"Then the offspring of Israel also will cease
From being a nation before Me forever."
    (Jeremiah 31:35-36)

God has always been orderly, and we are called to mirror His image. The Lord doesn't want our search for truth to be a shot in the dark. The study of Scripture should be intentional. My pantry? Random. The socks I pair up because I don't want the leftovers? Random. Bible study?

Deliberate.

At other times the Bible is approached as a quick fix. We end up with four and a half free minutes between Special K Red Berries and yet another packed morning, so we throw open our Bibles and scavenge an upper for the day: "Let's see . . . I just need one happy little truth to keep me nice today. I'll look up a verse on kindness. No. Longsuffering!" We use the Bible for a jolt of godliness, like a triple-shot espresso from Starbucks. If asked later, we'd smile piously and answer, "Of course I had Bible study today. Didn't you notice how especially longsuffering I was being?"

One psalmist asked,

> How can a young man keep his way pure?
> By keeping it according to Your word.
> *With all my heart* I have sought You. (119:9-10)

How much of our hearts seek after the Father when we grant His very Word five minutes of our day?

We pour our hearts into every other activity deemed worthy. For instance, after a years-long obsession with Home & Garden Television, I lost accountability for six entire months after we moved into our house. My memory is blurred with sage-painted cabinets and Home Depot bills. Were it not for the decided absence of paychecks, it was practically a full-time job for a while.

We've committed untold hours to the temporary and stamped ourselves "busy," yet we find it taxing to be in the Word for more than a few minutes. Can God speak to us through a quick Scripture reference? Of course. He's God. He's used to working in spite of us. Plus, there are times when He asks for only a moment of our time to impart a word. But "the eyes of the LORD move to and fro throughout the earth that He may strongly support *those whose heart is completely His*" (2 Chronicles 16:9). The five-minute heart may get a thought for the day, but when it comes to intimately knowing God, understanding the significance of His Word, and diving into Truth, it will be the all-my-heart believer who will come away changed.

Often, it's not time limits we place on Bible study but subject limits. We get stuck seeking out tag words we want to hear about (grace, love, loopholes to submission). After I taught these concepts to college girls at the University of Texas, one gal—I'll call her Cute and Thin Girl—approached me. She said, "When I read the Bible, I look up verses about dating from my concordance in the back. Sometimes I branch out and look up verses on gossiping." Well, to her credit, she will probably have the least dysfunctional college romance, requiring little to no therapy, and she has likely refrained from spreading at least half the dirt on her sorority sisters than she would have. Those may not become her problem areas, but there's a chance there is more to life than boys and rumors (a small chance, but a chance nonetheless).

But like her, many of us spend time in the Word that is marked by narrow reading. We seek out what we want to know. Now, is this a bad idea under any circumstance? Certainly not. We *should* fill our minds with God's truth in the specific areas under attack in our lives. If we are battling for purity, surrounding ourselves with Scriptures on holiness is a strategy for victory. Bedding down with a theme for a season is appropriate.

The danger comes in always and only reading like this. Beyond what we want to learn, what about what God wants us to learn? By definition, limited input can produce only limited spiritual growth. I once spent an obsessive amount of time looking up verses on worry, but it wasn't until God coaxed me into reading actual examples of His power that I was freed.

And don't even get me started on all the times God has led me at His discretion, calling attention to nasty places in my heart that I wasn't aware of. No one has a better handle on the true state of our souls than God does, though we compete with His wisdom. He sees the big picture of who we are now and where we are going next. He wants to purify and prepare us, but how can He lead us completely if all we'll read are verses on forgiveness? The Bible was not meant to be simply a reactive tool to use as we see fit. We think we know what we need to hear, but God alone is wise. We would do well to follow the psalmist's example:

> I rise before dawn and cry for help;
> I wait for Your words. (119:147)

A similar pitfall is limiting Scripture to what is easy or familiar. We reach a comfort level with a book or section and decide to camp out there for a while—or forever. Let's face it: Some parts of the Bible are easier to read. I can rifle through James like a woman possessed, but wading through the Minor Prophets? That's really going to make me think, and I'm not sure I'm up for it. Plus, what's with all that judgment? I'm pretty sure I don't want to know about that. Where are the verses on grace?

We are drawn back to favorite sections like a safe, secure crutch we can lean on. It makes sense there. All the verses have been previously underlined. There are already notes in the margins. Much less is required of us on the roads we've traveled before. We are creatures of comfort, and blazing through the roads less traveled can be decidedly bumpy.

Now, before you throw this book in the fireplace and curse its ashes, let me say this about familiar Scriptures: We all—myself included—have treasured passages that are uniquely meaningful. Often those pages are wrinkled with wear, and the print is so faded that you'd be uncertain if it said "be diligent" or "be degenerate" if you hadn't read it ten million times already.

Rereading not only reminds us where we've journeyed

but also compels us to remember the Shepherd who led us. That is a credit to our wonderful God, who can take His Word to the masses and transform it into a prize for the individual heart. By all means, reread your treasures. Love them. Remember them. Learn fresh truths from them. Memorize them. The psalmist said,

> Your word I *have treasured* in my heart,
> That I may not sin against You. (119:11)

To be sure, His Word is living, and the significance of a passage can change many times as we read it again and again.

That is fine and good and wonderful.

Again, the problem comes in reading only well-known verses without embracing unfamiliar Scripture. God's Word is a canvas of many colors. If we choose only to recognize the blues and greens, we'll miss all the reds and purples. There have been times I've stubbornly stuck to themes in Scripture (such as happiness and blessings and laughter and dancing) while God was waiting to teach me about being *stubborn*. Sometimes I give Him chest pains.

The Bible—all of it—is a catalyst for change. God asks us in Jeremiah 23:29, "Is not My word like fire . . . and like a hammer which shatters a rock?" We cannot be fully refined for His purposes or broken for His holiness if we submit only to the parts of Scripture we can easily comprehend. If we never choose to be stretched, then we choose to become stagnant. "*Every* word of God is tested" (Proverbs 30:5) and can mature us if we will decide to read each one.

Limited study not only hinders spiritual growth but also confines our perception of the Lord. Reading portions of the

Bible (What is this extraneous section in the first two-thirds of the book labeled Old Testament?) puts boundaries around the characteristics of God we are exposed to. If we read only about God's mercy, we don't gain an accurate understanding of His power. If we read only New Testament accounts of His faithfulness, we miss the miracles He orchestrated before Jesus arrived on the scene.

Think of it like this: If you spent time with me only in the 6:30 to 7:30 a.m. block of the day, there is a strong chance you would consider me unstable and slightly neurotic. You'd make up excuses to stay away from me and put me on multiple prayer lists for the disturbed. But if you came around after the second cup of coffee was absorbed into my bloodstream, you might find me downright pleasant. You might take me off the prayer lists, but that remains a question mark. If you came before I had my coffee, you wouldn't get a complete picture of who I really am. There is more to me than that small time frame suggests, but you have to stick around long enough to learn that (but who could blame you for not staying, really?).

By the same token, God and His Word are multifaceted and require a complete embrace if we are seeking a true knowledge of who He is. The psalmist points out,

> The *sum* of Your word is truth,
> And every one of Your righteous ordinances is
>   everlasting. (119:160)

Though I believe math is a tool of the Enemy, I learned enough to know that to accurately find the sum, you add up all the parts.

One of the Bible study approaches that has plagued most of us is reading the Word passively with no interaction, questioning, or communication. We open the Bible up, read way too much Scripture, take the parts we understand at face value, ignore the rest, and close it up. Done. Check it off the list. Strangely enough, most of it has dissipated by noon, and we couldn't confirm that we read anything at all by bedtime.

Girls, God's Word is ignited by processing it with Him deliberately. The psalmist prays,

Blessed are You, O LORD;
Teach me Your statutes . . . .
Open my eyes, that I may behold
Wonderful things from Your law. (119:12,18)

As God leads us, we are to be actively engaged in understanding His truth.

Case in point: Recently, I was sitting near two college students who were working on advanced calculus in Starbucks. (Yes, I was eavesdropping. So? You've done it.) One of them was clearly smarter than the other. He was spouting off formulas and talking smarty-pants language that, quite frankly, he was probably making up. I wasn't impressed. I already told you how I feel about Smarter People, and it's compounded exponentially when they are younger than I am.

The Smart One was trying to explain some complicated calculatory problem to the Not As Smart One. He was ranting and writing things down, and ridiculous words were gushing out of his mouth. Were it not for the occasional insertion of "and" or "then," I'd have mistaken it for a foreign language. Five minutes into this explanation, he glanced up at his protégé, and she was visiting another planet. She was as glazed over as I am when my sweet husband talks to me about sticking to our budget.

He threw down his pencil in frustration, knowing that not a word of his dissertation had made it past her skull into brain matter. "I'm not going to explain this if you don't pay attention! This is complicated!" he hollered at her. I'll say. That's what you get for being a math major. No sympathies. But she skidded back to earth with apologies and excuses about sleep deprivation and attention disorders. Sure. She was just bored like the rest of us who were eavesdropping.

But on the second pass, her behavior was different. She was pointing and writing and asking questions every eight seconds. She was fully engaged in the calculatory process this time. And lo and behold, guess who figured out the problem? Not As Smart One might turn into Marginally Smart after all. Once their exchange converted from a lecture to a conversation, she understood the numbers in front of her.

We need to think about Bible study as a conversation. To fully understand it, we must respond to it. That's where the real exchange begins. God is infinitely willing to explain it to us, but are we ready to engage? After all, it can be complicated, and we need a Navigator who is smarter than we are. (By the way, my spell-checker refuses to accept *calculatory* as a word, but it's not the boss of me. The word stands.)

I want to mention something else, though it pains me to do so. The books we buy at the Christian bookstore that are written by magnificent authors do not count as Bible study. I'm sorry. Many believers get together to discuss a great book and mistakenly call it Bible study. That is, in fact, a book club with a spiritual theme. Even if an author references Scripture, her book does not make the cut for authentic time in the Word. I honestly wish it did sometimes. Books require less of me, and the path of least resistance is an old and dear friend of mine.

Do we love some of our Christian authors? Well, land sakes, I sure hope so. Books are a wonderful way to fuel our beliefs and advance our faith, but they are an enrichment tool, not a substitution for God's Word. And to be sure, topical books will take on the style and opinions of the author. One book on Christian living will have an entirely different slant than another on the same topic. Discerning between truth and truth mixed with opinion can be daunting at best and downright misleading at worst.

What is true?

As Jesus prayed for all future believers, He said, "Sanctify them in the truth; Your *word* is truth" (John 17:17). At the end of the day, God's Word is the only real deal. Period. Jesus couldn't be clearer: "If you continue in *My word*, then you are truly disciples of Mine; and you will know the truth, and the truth will make you free" (8:31-32). Girls, is the Bible enough for you?

It can be.

Any combination of these faulty approaches will lead to the biggest pitfall of all: inconsistency. I don't know a single believer (well, maybe a few, but I don't really like them) who hasn't struggled with maintaining a regular commitment to the Bible. For most, dedication comes in waves cresting and falling on inconsistent factors. We're in it for a ten-week group Bible study; we're out of it for the four-week break. We're on from January 1 to February 8; we're off because we hit Deuteronomy.

Rats.

This was always my biggest frustration. I came crawling back to God countless times with the same intro: "Hi. I guess You haven't heard from me in a few weeks/months." Why couldn't I stick with it? I surely loved God. I truly wanted to live a life that reflected Jesus. I even knew the Bible was my only shot at hitting that target. What was my problem? Bless Paul for saying, "For what I am doing, I do not understand; for I am not practicing what I would like to do, but I am doing the very thing I hate" (Romans 7:15).

I hear you, Paul.

I figured it out: The problem was my methods. All these approaches to the Word—used exclusively—did not breed a burning passion for God's Word. They didn't leave me breathless with excitement or starving for more. Rather, they left me shrugging. "Hmmm. Okay. I guess that's it, then." And inevitably I'd quit reading.

Girls, when the power of God's Word is cracked open, you cannot stay out of it. Your soul will starve without it. Bible study becomes a function of necessity rather than obligation. I mean it. Don't cross your arms and roll your eyes. I'm not talking churchy talk for the elite. This is true for everyone willing to risk the journey. There is a way to spend time with God in His Word for a lifetime of fulfillment, consistency, and understanding.

If you've practiced any of these approaches to the Word and been left empty-handed, take heart. First of all, you are not alone. Brand-new believers to the most seasoned churchgoers have thrown in the towel. Falling in love with God's Word sometimes seems like a romantic notion for the mature, doesn't it?

Give me a little more of your time. My goal is to arm you with simple (really) strategies for making the Bible leap to life. It won't be complicated. It won't involve colored overlays or geometric diagramming. It will not cause abnormal anxiety or contribute to ulcers. This is not a book for the Holy Huddle of the Righteous but for regular believers who want to begin a love affair with God's Word.

No one wants that for you more than your Savior.

For this commandment which I command you today is not too difficult for you, nor is it out of reach. It is not in heaven, that you should say, "Who will go up to heaven for us to get it for us and make us hear it, that we may observe it?" Nor is it beyond the sea, that you should say, "Who will cross the sea for us to get it for us and make us hear it, that we may observe it?" But the word is very near you, in your mouth and in your heart, that you may observe it. See, I have set before you today life and prosperity. (Deuteronomy 30:11-15)

Codependency That Doesn't Require Therapy

Learning to Lean on the Holy Spirit

A few years ago, I discovered an obscure cooking show. I watched it only two or three times (lest you're judging me for watching TV in the middle of the day when I should have had better things to do, such as scrubbing stains out of the carpet or practicing being spiritual). Plus, I found it when I was channel surfing while nursing yet another baby, which, as far as I can tell, was all I actually got done during my twenties.

This show was my worst nightmare. A chef would appear on some unsuspecting soul's doorstep and barge in, intent on cooking a gourmet meal with whatever was in her kitchen. I'm certain this dog-and-pony show was contrived, because I never saw one pair of dirty underwear hanging on a banister or a single disheveled child barging into the kitchen for milk (if he was the first child) or Coke (if she was the third). A taping at our house would have ended up almost entirely on the cutting room floor with just two minutes of usable footage, but I digress.

He'd rummage around the kitchen and pull this ingredient out to mix with that one. The ruse continued as he'd ask, "Do you have any fresh rosemary? Cheerio! [He was a Brit.] Here it is!" Who has that, I ask you? In my kitchen, he would've found half a box of Cocoa Puffs and a bag of frozen peas. Good luck with that.

By the end, he'd set the polished, clutter-free table (dog-and-pony show confirmation) with a delicious meal from appetizers to dessert. "Was all this in there?" the family would gasp. They'd eat and gush and wonder why these flavors had never come out of their kitchen if supposedly they were in there to begin with. The chef would end with something clever and British and skip out the door, leaving the family in culinary (if temporary) bliss.

Would you believe that you already have everything you need to study the Bible with discernment? You don't need a workbook. You don't need a video. You don't need a tutor. You have the necessary ingredients, but perhaps you haven't learned to combine them properly. With a few nudges in the right direction, you would be amazed at your very own time in the Word.

If not me, would you believe God? He tells us in 2 Peter 1:3, "His divine power has given us *everything we need* for life and godliness through our knowledge of him who called us by his own glory and goodness" (NIV). Everything? Is that a misprint? How?

Girls, Scripture is clear: "through our knowledge of him." So the question becomes this: Where does your knowledge of Him come from? Does it depend *solely* on what someone else tells you? Many believers know God only as He is known by their teachers. Various passages mean this or that based on the interpretations we've heard or read somewhere. Verses become meaningful because they were to someone else. Notes in the margins are another person's words.

Those insights are valuable, but do you comprehend that God has understanding available for *you*? On your own. By yourself. He hasn't set apart favorites to grant insight to while the rest of us flounder around and wait for them to share the mysteries.

Look at God's history: He took His salvation, His Holy Spirit, His Word, and His rewards from His very own people exclusively—Israel—and shared them with all who believe because of His great love. Peter put it best in Acts 10:34: "I most certainly understand now that God is not one to show partiality." If He didn't reserve salvation for the privileged, why would He reserve knowledge?

God offers revelation to every believer through the perfection of His Word. Why? He told us in Proverbs 19:2, "It is not good to have zeal without knowledge" (NIV). *It's not good.* By default, it's *so* good to educate your passion. A life set on fire begins in the heart and burns out of control in the head. God desires a personal connection with every believer who calls Him Father, and knowledge of Him fuels that flame. This is nothing to panic about. This is God's design.

To that end, He offers us His Word.

God's Word *is* who He is.

We gain no greater knowledge of God than encountering Him verse by verse.

Reality Bites

I studied education at Oklahoma Baptist University (for the salary obviously). Through no fault of my own, I was born totally Type A. So between "studying" with Brandon, girl-friend nonsense, and my social calendar, I graduated magna cum laude, to which my genetics predisposed me in the womb. We firstborns succeed only because we desperately need approval, which has been a cute little sticking point with me and God. Apparently that's not biblical or something. Coincidentally, Brandon had more fun in college than I did and labeled himself at graduation "Hakuna Matata"—no worries.

I mostly paid attention in class, and I never missed an assignment (because I needed the approval of my professors, of course). They stamped me "Prepared for Life and Well Educated" and released me to instruct the young and impressionable.

I was soon hired to teach fourth grade at Jenks East Elementary in Tulsa. I had four years of college under my belt, so clearly I was equipped to be a killer teacher. I was sure those theories and progressive strategies were going to change education as we knew it. The students would be perfect, my teaching would be astonishing, birds would light on my shoulder, and people would break out in song. I would probably win at least one award.

Two weeks before school started, I walked into my class-room toting a box of teaching stuff from college that mostly didn't apply to fourth grade. And let's not forget the seventy-five-dollar check I got from the district to spend on supplies for the entire year.

Basically, I had nothing.

But there were papers everywhere: class lists, bus duty schedules, rules, required skills for every subject, cafeteria policies, volunteer vacancies, assessment deadlines. The sheer reality of the requirements left me twitching like the deranged and considering a liquor habit.

My dear Teammate Sandy found me sitting on the floor surrounded by the stacks and crying like a toddler, "I have no idea what to do! Why did they give me a degree? How am I supposed to be in charge of thirty kids next week? Has the whole world gone mad?" She talked me down off the ledge and managed to stop me from ripping my contract to shreds.

It was not one of my finer moments.

Isn't it true that we can hear all *about* the Bible, listen to godly counsel about reading it, and watch other people fall in love with it, but when it's time to encounter the Word by ourselves, we look around in shock, wondering who thought we were equipped to do that? When it comes to studying the Bible, being a hearer is much easier than being a doer. The reality of being alone with God's Word—not in mechanical reading but for significance—sometimes freaks us out.

The Three-Legged Approach

My Girlfriend Trina advocates the three-legged approach to parenting: threatening, bribing, and screaming. It's a genius strategy that I once employed with questionable discernment in the middle of Target when my daughter bit her six-month-old brother on the leg for touching her, and I spent the next week terrified that the security tape had been sent to Child

Protective Services and my children would be raised by foster parents while I spent the rest of my life in anger management classes. No one came knocking, but I didn't go to Target for a month, which is a miracle on par with the Virgin Birth.

Well, guess what? God adheres to a three-legged approach to Bible study: you, the Word, and the Holy Spirit. My friend, you are not alone. God knows better than that. This is the same God who calls us sheep, known for neither brilliance nor intuitiveness. He didn't craft His magnificent Word only to toss it down and shout over His shoulder, "Good luck with that. Let Me know how that works out for you." The God of the universe knows that our ability to wrap human arms around His Word is completely inadequate.

A Little Help?

Jesus promised, "The Helper, the Holy Spirit, whom the Father will send in My name, He will teach you all things, and bring to your remembrance all that I said to you" (John 14:26). Another way has been made. Help has arrived. Helper is the Greek word *paraklētos*, which means "advisor, exhorter, comforter, strengthener, interceder, encourager, and teacher."[1] We don't have to wade through Scripture relying on our own merits or lack thereof. We have a Personal Tutor to guide us through every verse.

That is one of His primary functions.

The Holy Spirit has a long history with the Bible. It was through His supernatural leadership that Scripture was written in the first place. Peter tells us that "no prophecy was ever made by an act of human will, but men moved by the Holy Spirit spoke from God" (2 Peter 1:21). Neither the writing nor the understanding of Scripture was ever possible without His guidance. At the intersection of God's Word and mankind, human understanding has never been a deciding factor.

What does this mean? What is this guidance? Can we turn up the volume on this leadership? I admit I'm not a girl in tune with the subtle stuff. My Bible Study Friend Leah senses God in the slightest changes or "check in her spirit," as she says. I look around and wonder if the air conditioner kicked on. "What? What did you pick up on?" I'm always bewildered. I have no sensitivity whatsoever. God deals with me in large, demonstrative motions the deaf and blind could interpret. I respond to that. But Leah is on to something.

The Holy Spirit often deals in subtlety.

I love the story of Elijah, but my favorite part is when he was disheartened and running for his life (stick with me), and the Lord revealed Himself on Mount Horeb. Elijah was at the end of hope and had never needed God's presence like he did then. He had obeyed God completely and journeyed exactly where God told him to go. Yet God still asked him as he sat hiding in a cave, "What are you doing here, Elijah?" (1 Kings 19:9).

Elijah responded honestly, "I've loved You so much, God, but I feel alone. Where are You?" God used this moment to teach Elijah—and us—a sweet lesson on His presence. He called Elijah out on the mountain, and 1 Kings 19:11-12 says,

> Behold, the LORD was passing by! And a great and strong wind was rending the mountains and breaking in pieces the rocks before the LORD; but the LORD was not in the wind. And after the wind an earthquake, but the LORD was not in the earthquake. After the

earthquake a fire, but the LORD was not in the fire; and after the fire a sound of a gentle blowing.

There He was. He'd been there all along.

Girls, this is a beautiful word picture of the Holy Spirit walking beside us in gentleness. We've trained our heads to jerk toward the roaring winds and thunderous earthquakes but haven't learned to discern the Holy Spirit's whisperings. We often feel alone in God's Word, but the Spirit stands ready to guide us through it tenderly.

Careful . . .

There is another danger to wading through Scripture without the Helper. Not only could we emerge confused, but in the absence of God-appointed leadership, we are also at risk of making up our own interpretations. The Holy Spirit directs our hearts into truth. He protects us from misinterpretation and outright deception. As Paul explained, "The thoughts of God no one knows except the Spirit of God. Now we have received, not the spirit of the world, but the Spirit who is from God, so that we may know the things freely given to us by God, which things we also speak, not in words taught by human wisdom, but in those taught by the Spirit" (1 Corinthians 2:11-13).

Make no mistake: The spirit of this world loves it when believers decipher Scripture in their own wisdom. Much carnage has come from this approach. When man interprets Scripture solely as he sees fit, he becomes like those Paul described in Romans 1:21,25: "For even though they knew God, they did not honor Him as God or give thanks, but they became futile in their speculations, and their foolish heart was darkened. . . . For they exchanged the truth of God for a lie."

Some misinterpret Scripture intentionally to suit their agendas, but other believers are deceived simply by omitting the Holy Spirit from their journey. Jeremiah tells us,

> The heart is more deceitful than all else
> And is desperately sick. (Jeremiah 17:9)

On its own, the heart can turn what the Lord intended for godliness into a tool for the Liar. Scripture has been misinterpreted, exploited for personal gain, used for unmerited justification, and employed in judgment of others when unchecked by the Holy Spirit. We are just not capable or wise enough to read it on our own.

Girls, God's Word is a "two-edged sword" (Hebrews 4:12). It will be wielded powerfully, whether in truth or in deception. It is imperative for our knowledge and safety that we learn to listen to the Holy Spirit when we encounter the Word.

The Spirit is the Person of the Trinity who teaches us, inspires us, grants us understanding, and carries us to completion, but He gets the least attention. We pledge our devotion to God and praise the sacrifice of Jesus, as well we should, but we rarely think intimately about the Holy Spirit. We even refer to Him as an it, as if He were some intangible idea. Just as surely as God wants to adore us and Jesus wants to redeem us, the Holy Spirit wants to teach us.

How Do I Plug In?

Learning to hear Him begins with acknowledging who He is and what He desires to accomplish. Which is . . . what? Jesus said, "When He, the Spirit of truth, comes, He will guide you into all the truth . . . and He will disclose to you what is to come" (John 16:13). Raise your hand if you want to be guided into truth. Raise your hand if you want things disclosed to you. (If you're really raising your hand, put it down. People are going to laugh at you. I wasn't being literal.)

It begins simply enough. Have a frank conversation with the Holy Spirit. Tell Him your frustrations with the Word. Don't hold anything back, because He is the Teacher whose existence centers around His students. Why? He wants more for our lives than we could ever wish for.

He comes to school early and stays late to tutor. (Truth be told, He lives there—which is what we always suspected of our teachers in grade school.) He patiently stands over each student's shoulder, pointing out strategies and correcting errors. He listens to questions and crafts answers to meet each need. His students call Him confidently at all hours, knowing His desire for their success. All students receive the Teacher's undivided attention no matter how remedial they are—in fact, the slow ones get an extra hand. He encourages every student constantly in struggles and achievements.

Why does He do this? Why does He care so much? First, the Teacher loves His students—plain and simple. They've been entrusted to His care, and He jealously works for their advancement. Second, the success of His students is a direct reflection on Him. His classroom becomes larger as His fame spreads through the testimony of His students. He is able to train many more when word leaks out of His superior teaching style and patient manner.

Have a conference with the Teacher. Tell Him you'd like to be admitted to His class. Your transcript may be sketchy, and you may have spent a bit of time in detention for past shenanigans such as bailing on school for Senior Skip Day when your mom wouldn't call in sick for you, even though she knew everyone was just going to the Wichita Zoo. But you're in luck; the only requirement for admittance is to believe in Him.

Next, invite the Holy Spirit to meet you in the Word. His response to this is 100 percent because without Him, you're attempting the two-legged approach to Bible study and will end up on your backside, having lost your balance and confidence in the whole concept. We will talk about how and what to read in the rest of this book, but you might as well use those pages for kindling if you don't first ask the Holy Spirit to be your Teacher.

Every time.

No matter how familiar the passage is. No matter how much you think you know. Not just after you read (though that is also encouraged) but before.

Before.

"Holy Spirit, teach me what is true about these verses. What do You want me to understand? Direct my thoughts with every word I read. Protect and lead my mind." It's as simple as that. Proverbs 2:3-5 says,

> For if you cry for discernment,
> Lift your voice for understanding;
> If you seek her as silver

And search for her as for hidden treasures;
Then you will discern the fear of the LORD
And discover the knowledge of God.

I know with absolute certainty this passage is true. I begged for discernment after years of unproductive time in the Word. I agreed to open my Bible with a blank sheet of paper, a few strategies, and a plea for the Holy Spirit to teach me. Truly, it was like I was reading it for the first time.

The Holy Spirit answered me, and I fell in love with God's Word. Me. Not a Bible scholar. Not a seminary grad. Not a professional Christian. Just a regular believer with many obvious and disturbing issues who finally allowed God's intention for His Word to be realized in her.

And in case you think I'm a bit questionable (and who would blame you?), I've seen this same transformation happen in countless believers with just the Helper and a few simple study methods in their arsenal. From new Christians to veterans, women are encountering God's Word like never before. My Bible Study Friend Christi says she can't get her nose out of the Bible and has taken her husband's Bible hostage as an additional tool. While this book is not designed to cause marital strain, my prayer is that it will forever change the way you feel about God's Word.

The remainder of this book will put strategies in your hands that will help you listen and respond to the gentle whispers of the Helper. It takes a little practice, but you can place your success in the safekeeping of the Holy Spirit, who has sealed us in faith and leads us in victory. God promises us, "I will put My Spirit within you and *you will come to life*" (Ezekiel 37:14).

"Things which eye has not seen and ear has not heard, and which have not entered the heart of man, *all that* God has prepared for those who love Him." For to us God revealed them through the Spirit; for the Spirit searches all things, even the depths of God. (1 Corinthians 2:9-10)

* * * CHAPTER 4 * * *

The Container-Store Theory

Every Mess Can Be Organized

For my mental health, I've repressed nearly all experiences from junior high. Those years are typically not kind to us girls. Tragically, I entered this phase in the mideighties when I believed a five-inch tidal wave of bangs with matching wings would conceal my gawkiness and distressing lack of boobs. Not pretty. Thankfully, most of those memories have fallen into the abyss, leaving only remnants of irrational insecurities and vague notions of rejection.

However, I clearly remember the wonderful new world of talking on the phone. The wonderful new world of boys was mixed in there too, but most of those memories qualify for the rejection abyss. My seventh grade treasure was a tacky, hot pink phone with oversized buttons. The beauty of this phone—outside its obvious external merits—was its location: my bedroom. It's a wonder I ever came out of there.

Talking on the phone in those years landed in two distinct camps: talking to girls and talking to boys. In the boy department, I employed at least two equally Aqua-Netted girlfriends to feed me topic prompts. With our three bangs and six wings, we were a walking freak show with the ability to slice your eyes out with one quick hair jab if you spoke an ugly word about Duran Duran or our frosted lipstick.

Together, we'd call the victim. Phone conversations with those boys could be summed up in two words: painful and brief. Were it not for the occasional grunt on the other end, I'd have thought for sure our connection had been lost. After I'd exhausted my girlfriends' ideas and sat in silence for as long as I could handle, I'd finally end his misery and hang up.

Now, talking to girls was a different experience entirely. I'd tie up the phone line for hours, as girls were willing to indulge my ramblings about Sadie Hawkins dances and cheerleading tryouts. The rest of my family would wait for the phone indefinitely, assuming I'd eventually have to come up for air. As if. The seventh grade girl is awkward on nearly every front, but she can talk on the phone with unmatched skill and longevity. Sadly, I really wanted to talk to the boys, but they were too immersed in their bizarre voice mutations and social deficiencies. The few times I did get through probably scarred them for life.

As God's children, we fall into one of those two camps. God has extended a lifetime of communication to us through the Bible and the Spirit who leads us. Some of us are fully interacting with Him in the Scriptures, and the phone lines are tied up for hours. There is much give and take with both ends talking, listening, and responding. These conversations within the Word have become a wonderful new world of friendship and intimacy.

But most of us fall somewhere in the other camp. Communication is largely one-sided, with our end marked by awkward silence and brevity. It's not for lack of desire that these scriptural connections are unproductive, because God certainly plans to speak for hours on end with every believer. But how far can that relationship advance when we refuse to engage? God has spoken clearly to us through His Word and Holy Spirit, but our fears, insecurities, and ignorance have kept us silent and unattached.

The Gimpy Leg

The three-legged approach—you, the Word, and the Holy Spirit—has only one weak leg. Two of them are money in the bank. To date, they have never buckled or proven remotely faulty.

In terms of God's Word, Psalm 18:30 sums it up perfectly:

As for God, His way is blameless;
The word of the LORD is tried.

Only absolute truth could transcend every culture, age group, and race over some two thousand years. If the Bible were a calculated scam full of fiction and unfounded promises, we'd know it by now, wouldn't we? After millions of brilliant minds have studied, researched, dissected, and evaluated God's Word for the last two millennia, its perfection stands as the most published and purchased book in history.

Concerning the Holy Spirit, God's promise is clear in Ezekiel 36:27: "*I will put My Spirit within you* and cause you to walk in My statutes." The Holy Spirit is a constant inner presence who will guide us moment by moment if we listen. Jesus said of the Spirit in John 16:14, "He will glorify Me, for He will take of Mine and will *disclose it to you.*" God's Word and Spirit are perfect. My pastor would say they are "sweet brown sugar."

That leaves the precarious third leg: us. We remain the only possible factor to make authentic Bible study ineffective. Studying God's Word is a perfect example of Philippians 2:12-13, where Paul tells us to "work out your salvation with fear and trembling; for it is God who is at work in you, both to will and to work for His good pleasure."

Living life as the rescued demands a response: work. We must do our part to grow beyond salvation by allowing what began in our hearts to infect our minds. Never fear, God will "work in" us throughout the entire journey, as the Creator is well acquainted with our questionable habits and propensity to wander, but we have to respond with due diligence.

My youngest son, Caleb, is a reckless teenage boy trapped in a toddler's body. Truly. He's a man-child who at thirteen months of age donned his big brother's Nikes, opened our front door, walked down the street, and let himself into our neighbors' backyard (unlatching their gate, naturally) for a romp on their trampoline while I thought he was napping. *Thirteen months old.* My daily goal is to keep him alive.

When it suits his agenda, he announces that he is big and has put the world of baby-type things behind him, such as snuggling and good eating habits. When he strives for independence, we usually stand back and let him spread his wings because, truthfully, we're all a little scared of him.

But wouldn't you know, when I want him to do things that don't fit his liking (and they are legion), he tells me with impressive boy drama, "I can't do that. I'm too little." I see. He has mastered manipulation at the preschool level, and frankly I'm terrified. See, he's big when it suits him and little when being big becomes uncomfortable.

Sound familiar?

We often flash our faith proudly when doing so suits the moment. We girls can talk a Christian game like nobody's business. You'd think we came straight from the lineage of Jesus and maybe wrote a book or two of the Bible by the way we talk. But wait. Spend time studying the Bible? Every day? By *myself*? I'm too little.

It is our responsibility to grow up in the Word. It will not happen in a vacuum. It doesn't come from a gratuitous wave of God's Maturity Wand. It requires time and work as we team up with the Holy Spirit. Hebrews 5:12-14 sheds truth on our responsibility to God's Word:

> In fact, though by this time you ought to be teachers, you need someone to teach you the elementary truths of God's word all over again. You need milk, not solid food! Anyone who lives on milk, being still an infant, is not acquainted with the teaching about righteousness. But solid food is for the mature, who *by constant use* have trained themselves to distinguish good from evil. (NIV)

Whoa. That's a serious helpin' of straight talk written to the *whole church*—not just the leaders. Was it intended for the varsity Christians who had earned patches and merit badges? No. There was nobody like that. Faith in Jesus was brand-new.

God is saying that He desires biblical maturity for and from every believer, regardless of how long they've been in the Club. But we so often prefer infancy, don't we? It requires much less from us, and there's always someone else to spoon-feed us what we need.

This passage tells us two important things. One, those who choose to remain in infancy are "not acquainted" properly with God's Word. Not acquainted with its power. Not acquainted with its relevance. Not acquainted with its Helper. There lurks an element of ignorance surrounding the Bible.

Two, those who *are* striving for maturity have been trained in the Word by "constant use." They are all-my-heart lovers of the Bible. By default, *occasional* use of the Word will keep us on the bottle forever because our spiritual health hasn't been nourished enough to enable a transition to solid food. The perfect design of constant use is that it creates a hunger for more Scripture. When well fed, our biblical appetites not only grow but also enable our systems to digest stronger truths. Now, some of you got hung up on "by this time you ought to be teachers" in verse 12. You became queasy and thought you might throw up for a second. Becoming mature in God's Word does not mean you will be preaching in your pastor's absence or joining the Christian speakers' circuit. But make no mistake: Every believer is a teacher.

We teach our children. We teach our spouses. We teach our friends, our neighbors, our coworkers, our church families, our parents, our sisters, and our brothers. The question is this: What are you teaching them? Are you impacting their lives with the solid food of God's Word, or are you losing precious, *precious* time because you have nothing to say?

How do we manage God's Word in obedience?

The best way I have discovered to engage my mind with Scripture is by becoming "acquainted" with God's Word by "constant use" through structured Scripture reading and focused journaling. What does that mean? I'm glad you asked.

Write On

I want to touch on journaling first. I realize the word *journaling* hits you in one of two ways. Some of you are inherent writers. You fill notebooks, e-mails, journals, margins, workbooks, and scrapbooks with volumes of personal thoughts. Writing comes naturally, and you tend to use flowery phrases and a disproportionate amount of adverbs.

I hear you. I love words. I talk too much and write using too many words (ask my editor). What should take the normal person a page and a half takes me a notebook. God wired writers this way. Don't judge us. Try to indulge our penchant for drawn-out rants and adjectives.

Now, others of you . . . not so much. You're more like my Girlfriend Trina, who when first approached about journaling could scarcely contain her eye rolling and gagging noises. (She has since become quite the journal advocate, which is hilarious to us.) But for you who are like Trina, journaling conjures up images of dramatic, ninth grade diary entries and hand cramps. You write checks. You sign your speeding tickets. You don't do journal entries.

I hear you, too. The last thing I want to produce is a book of strategies for writers only. That's a very small group of people marked by a tendency to grossly exaggerate and take credit for things they've heard their friends say.

So why journal? It goes back to the notion of engagement.

Let's think again about the study of the Bible as a conversation. In some ways, I'm a little jealous of the prophets—not so much of the imprisonments and whale encounters, but of the way God spoke to them in an audible voice, in vivid dreams, or through angels. Exodus 33:11 says, "The LORD used to speak to Moses face to face, just as a man speaks to his friend."

You would be hard-pressed to remain detached from the Lord with His thunderous voice rolling over your head. He spoke that way to accomplish His purposes through those chosen men. But God is "the same yesterday and today and forever" (Hebrews 13:8), and He's still talking, so how do we listen and respond today?

Journaling forces our minds to engage with the Holy Spirit in Scripture. We listen as we read; we respond as we write. It is a concrete way to talk back to God in the absence of His audible words and discernible body language. It focuses our attention on God's Word.

It's the difference between writing down a phone message when someone gives it to you and attempting the just-tell-me-and-I'll-remember method. Do I even need to mention how often that has backfired? (My husband wanted to insert a paragraph here. I told him to get his own book contract.) The Bible is a direct message of eternal significance. Journaling acknowledges that we care. It not only helps us retain Scripture more easily but also reveals to our Father that we are committed to "working out our salvation."

We'll do the work. We'll give the time. We'll offer our full attention.

Writing also allows us to process Scripture rather than read it briefly at face value. Often we begin a journal entry with one simple concept in mind, but as we write, our thoughts are carried to a deeper place by the Spirit. Why? Journaling requires us to consider a truth longer than the five seconds it took to read it. The Spirit's leadership pulls us along and stretches us as we journal because *writing equals time.*

It's not like I patented this idea. Long ago, God gave some written words to Moses on a mountain. Exodus 32:16 says, "The tablets were God's work, and the writing was *God's writing* engraved on the tablets." Likewise, after God delivered Israel from the tribe of Amalek, He told Moses, "*Write this* in a book as a memorial and recite it to Joshua" (Exodus 17:14). And again, God charged His people, "Fix these words of mine in your hearts and minds. . . . *Write them* on the doorframes of your houses and on your gates, so that your days and the days of your children may be many" (Deuteronomy 11:18,20-21, NIV).

Several other guys took to writing about God's influence in their lives: Joshua, Samuel, Jeremiah, David, Solomon, Isaiah, Daniel, Matthew, John, Paul, Peter, Luke, James. We have God's holy Word because they responded in obedience to write. Were they professional authors by trade? Sure, if you consider soldiers, tax collectors, and fishermen good candidates for novelists and biographers. They wrote out of submission to the God they loved, and He filled those words with truth through the Spirit who led them.

For you, journaling becomes a written legacy of your conversations with God as He leads you through His Word. It doesn't mean you churn out beautiful prose and poetic revelations. Besides new understanding, authentic journaling includes questions, frustrations, arguments, struggles, and doubts—the components of a real relationship.

Journaling comes from the same root word as *journey.* Doesn't that make sense? Writing is a tangible tool to connect with God as you travel from infancy to maturity. It isn't a glossy masterpiece fit for publishing, but it chronicles a journey through truth between two dear friends who constantly talk back and forth about what is real and what is true.

It says, "Here I am, Lord. Take me through Your Word."

Boundaries

So back to the structured part of the journey. I am aware that we are not all structure-oriented women. The Organized Club Members are often found reading books on parenting, marriage, or careers and immediately put into practice whatever is valuable. Their babies follow tight schedules, they hemorrhage cash on containers and labels to keep their homes in order, and they've mastered online banking.

And there are others who are, shall we say, more spontaneous? The boundaries are a bit looser, if not downright absent. Their babies drink Sprite while watching *Late Night with Conan O'Brian,* labels have always been considered "too establishment," and they pay bills when they feel the urge to do so (or the electricity is turned off).

I can say with confidence that these two orders of civilization can come together in regard to the Bible. The beauty of God's Word is that even when it is approached in an orderly fashion, it is still marked by freedom, surprises, and wide-open spaces. God's Word is a place where the by-the-book people and the I-didn't-know-there-was-a-book people can live in harmony.

Enough with the Random

My first suggestion about structure is to hang up the random method of opening the Bible and reading whatever you land on and instead choose a section to read from start to finish. Why? Context and themes stay intact, and information is protected from fragmentation. This will look a little different depending on where you're reading.

The New Testament is divided into books that are easy to read in start-to-finish segments. There are twenty-seven books in the New Testament, and twenty-one of them were written as letters (Romans through Jude). The books in letter form are best understood the same way they were written: in their entirety. Each book is a complete package in terms of the author, the audience, and the purpose. God set forth a specific message that resonates in unity throughout the entire book. Themes repeat and extend throughout all the chapters. We are likely (understatement of the century) to misunderstand Peter's teaching about submission in marriage in 1 Peter 3 if we don't first study Jesus' example in 1 Peter 2. Many truths are progressive, and each supporting detail builds upon the last.

The Gospels—Matthew, Mark, Luke, and John—are also perfect to read from beginning to end. There is no better way to encounter the life of Jesus than to read from the time He was born to the day He was resurrected. The gospels read like fascinating novels jam-packed with interesting characters and intense plot development.

The Old Testament is set up differently, though most books are still read best from start to finish. It is divided into four major sections:

- **The Law**: Genesis–Deuteronomy
- **History**: Joshua–Esther
- **Poetry and Wisdom**: Job–Song of Solomon
- **Prophets**: Isaiah–Malachi
  - During the divided kingdom (Israel in the north; Judah in the south): Obadiah, Joel, Jonah, Amos, Hosea, Isaiah, Micah
  - In Judah (after Israel's destruction): Nahum, Zephaniah, Jeremiah, Habakkuk
  - During the Exile: Daniel, Ezekiel, Lamentations
  - After the Exile: Haggai, Zechariah, Malachi

It is helpful to read the Old Testament chronologically, though in a twist of unfairness, it is not arranged in order but by genre. The chart on the next page gives the chronological order of Old Testament books, including those whose events took place at the same time.

As you can see, characters and plots are often spread out over several books, as many books cover the same time period. Reading them in chronological order establishes a secure understanding of Israel's obedience patterns (or lack thereof), relevant history, and changing relationship with God.

Sometimes the study of a character takes you to several books before you've read his entire history, and other times you pick up a character in the middle of a book. A quick glance in the index of your Bible will tell you where to begin reading about Noah, Job, Moses, Abraham, Isaac, Jacob, Joshua, Gideon, Ruth, Esther, Samuel, Saul, David, Jonathan, Solomon, Rahab, Elijah, Josiah, Nebuchadnezzar, Shadrach/Meshach/Abednego, Daniel, Jonah, Joseph. . . . The list goes

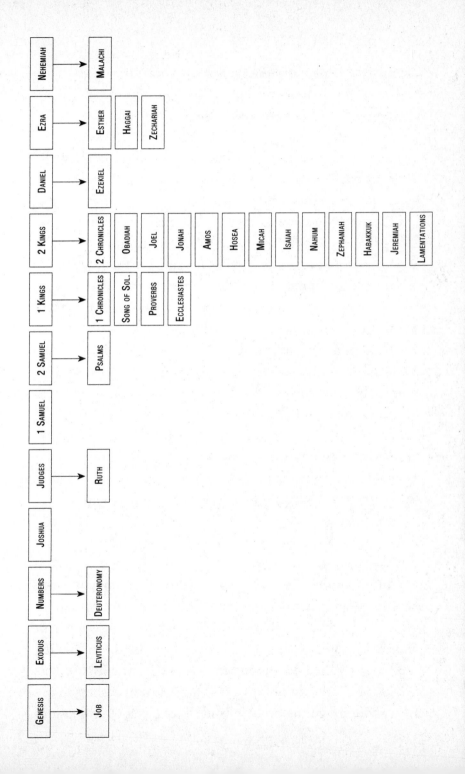

on, but those names alone will keep your nose in the Old Testament for so long you'll practically be a historian.

Here's the key: Read about these characters' lives from birth to death. Their stories aren't always tied up neatly in one book but are best understood when read completely.

The Prophets are rich with significance, history, and mercy. Granted, these can be more challenging to wade through, but they include some of the most poignant Scripture in the Bible. In these books we see a firsthand glimpse of God's great love for His people and His longing for their devotion. As much as they chronicle God's holiness, these books also demonstrate His compassion. Not to mention all that great prophecy about Jesus and the end times.

Themes of faithfulness, obedience, hope, and restoration are laced throughout every Old Testament book. Don't miss those. My Bible Study Friend Laura initially asked, "Who is this Old Testament God? He's very angry and picky." Keep reading. God's judgment constantly brought Israel back to Him. Restoration was never more than a word of repentance away. He still extended reckless love to His people though the perfect sacrifice had not yet been made for them.

I'm Overwhelmed. Where Do I Start?

My Bible Study Friend Amy pointed out the obvious literary discrepancy with reading the Bible. She assumed that, as with any good book, you start at the beginning: "It was a dark and stormy night" (for beach novels) or "In the beginning God created the heavens and the earth" (for the Bible). This works for about a book and a half until Exodus ushers in the laws about ox-goring protocol and thirty pages of dimensions for the tabernacle. Even the sturdiest Bible student can lose her resolve.

When you're ready to begin, I suggest starting in the Gospels. Luke is on my A-list, as it was written for a Gentile audience by the only Gentile author of the New Testament, but you *cannot* make a bad choice here. Begin with who matters most: Jesus. Camping out with Him during His life, death, and resurrection will ignite a passion in you for more of the Word. The rest of the Bible stands in juxtaposition to Jesus' ministry and purpose.

From there, read some of the smaller books in the New Testament, such as 1, 2, or 3 John or 1 or 2 Timothy. Bite off a chunk you can chew without involuntarily gagging and depositing your goods all over the floor. These are wonderful places to begin navigating Scripture and getting your legs under you.

When you're ready, try an Old Testament book, such as Esther or Ruth (plug for the girls) or Nehemiah. These are shorter books that tell amazing stories. They are simple to understand and have multiple points of application. If you are more systematic, begin reading the Old Testament in chronological order (which is helpful but not necessary). Otherwise, read the introduction to a few books to get a feel for the characters and events they describe and choose from there.

When in doubt, ask the Holy Spirit to lead you to a book, sit very still, and listen to His answer. By the time you've journaled through several books in the Bible, you will be ready to tackle those others you've skipped all your life. And guess what? You'll discover you love them, too.

When my small group began, we spent eight months journaling through 1 and 2 Peter, James, and Ephesians. We had gained such confidence in the Word that I decided we were ready for 1 Samuel. I pumped up my pitch and delivered the news with enthusiasm that could only be described as annoying. I received many blank stares, and I'm certain there was grumbling behind my back within minutes. So I became the Old Testament cheerleader for my Girlfriends. The troops were rallied and given cheesecake to squelch their dissension.

We dug in. We studied. We wrote. We talked. We took a serious trip through 1 Samuel. And lo and behold, there was legitimate mourning at the end of the book because our journey with Hannah, Eli, Samuel, Saul, David, Jonathan, and Abigail was over. Later, several of the girls informed me privately, "I would never have picked it on my own, but that book was for me."

And it was. It all is.

Less Is More

Once you've picked a place to start, the next obvious question is this: How much do I read each day? Our tendency is to read volumes of Scripture at a time. If we can read 125 pages of Nora Roberts in a sitting, why can't we handle four or five chapters of Acts? I sometimes think if I tackle that much, it makes me extra spiritual, and goodness knows I need someone to believe that about me.

Here's the thing about God's Word: Every verse is important. It is impossible to embrace all that is true about a passage if we read ten times as much as we can retain. For New Testament letters, I like to read ten verses or fewer per day. The focus is narrowed to a manageable chunk I can spend quality time with rather than barreling through thirty-five verses and remembering two.

For me, slow and steady wins the race — or at least doesn't come in dead last with a gimpy leg and dehydration issues. Many verses in the Bible seem less significant than some of their more obvious companions, but when given healthy attention, they can become some of the most insightful words from God we've read.

Most of the Old Testament books (and narratives such as the Gospels and Acts) can sustain larger daily divisions. But while you can certainly read more than five or six verses a day, they are still better digested in *smaller pieces*. There is much to learn from each decision made, every exchange with God, moments of obedience or disobedience, prayers offered up, or counsel sent down.

Here's a tip: Most Bibles divide each chapter into thematic segments. Natural breaks in content are labeled with subheadings that make daily reading a simple choice. I frequently follow those.

It boils down to this: Less is more. I think of it as the antithesis to my chips-and-salsa theory, which is "eat until your fingers are swollen with sodium and you're on the verge of throwing up." *Sometimes* too much of a good thing is a good thing — but not when it comes to Bible reading.

The key is slowing down.

My Girlfriend Andrea recently told me about a trip to Washington, D.C., to visit her father-in-law. She and her husband had never been there and had only three days for the trip. The entire city represents for a teenager a summer vacation gone dreadfully wrong and for a history nerd the fulfillment of every academic fantasy. As Andrea is married to a history nerd, they embarked on Mission Impossible: Embrace D.C. in three days.

She recounted driving around the city in the back of her in-laws' van, throwing open the sliding door while the vehicle was still moving. Her husband would dangle out of the van and take pictures. Without so much as hitting the brakes, they were off to the next "stop." The entire take-home value of her trip was reduced to a few sketchy pictures complete with blurry edges and half the van door.

What a different experience that trip would have been if she'd spent weeks in the city taking in the sights one place at a time. I realize that would mean weeks with the in-laws though, and there probably isn't enough historical value in the entire world to merit that kind of extended stay.

The Bible is like a spiritual Washington, D.C. (pardon the sacrilege—sometimes analogies require a bit of a stretch). It becomes more valuable and life changing when it is experienced deliberately over an extended period of time. Could you race through it? Sure, but all you'll end up with are blurry ideas and vague memories.

No Way Around It

My next suggestion has been around since man figured out there was a good God to spend time with. David was one who found it:

> It is good . . . to declare Your lovingkindness *in the morning.* (Psalm 92:1-2)

> O how I love Your law!

It is my meditation *all the day*. (119:97)

At midnight I shall rise to give thanks to You
Because of Your righteous ordinances.
  (119:62)

What does proficiency in God's Word require?

Time.

Now, believe me when I tell you that if anyone has tried to find a shortcut to knowing God more fully, it's me. If there were a way to mature that involved less exertion, I'd know about it. So take my pathetic word for it: Falling in love with God's Word requires consistent, extended time in it. Period. Anything else creates a glossy exterior with a large, vacant interior — and I'm speaking from experience.

It is possible to learn a great deal *about* the Bible while barely spending any personal time connecting with it. If you strung together all you'd ever heard in church, small groups, conferences, and Sunday school, you'd know a lot of stuff. However, the proof is in the pudding.

As Jesus told the Pharisees, who knew the Bible but not the Lord of the Bible, "Woe to you, scribes and Pharisees, hypocrites! For you are like whitewashed tombs which on the outside appear beautiful, but inside they are full of dead men's bones and all uncleanness" (Matthew 23:27). Spending time in the Word — with the Holy Spirit — is the only way to grow.

If you are like me in the slightest way, you might have thought, *Fewer verses to read per day? Less time!* Sorry to disappoint you. The key is less Scripture, more time.

My Girlfriend Stephanie has declared that, due to an unfortunate string of bad choices on her part, I am now in charge of making all decisions for her. Clearly this is the blind leading the blind, and at some point we will end up in a Mexican prison or on the Jerry Springer show. Likewise, I sense that you're asking, "How much time per day? Tell me a number. Make my decision. I need boundaries."

I can't. This is a moving target. It is going to look different from person to person, but I will *suggest* thirty minutes a day as a starting place. As your comfort level with Scripture and journaling grows, that time slot will probably grow as well. Can you imagine the benefits of spending thirty minutes with seven verses? We give the Holy Spirit the gift of time; He gives us more insight than we ever imagined.

Whatever this time frame initially looks like for you, one thing is sure: You absolutely must schedule it in. Amos 3:3 says, "Do two men walk together unless they have made an appointment?" Portions of my life, such as visits to the dentist and working out, are characterized by complete randomness, but I *schedule* date nights, salon time (if I was born blonde, I can only assume God intended for me to stay that way), coffee with girlfriends, events with my kids, and, yes, Bible study.

What do these things have in common? I care about them. They are important to me. I need them for sanity. They will get done because I want them to get done. This is the way life works. Don't even bother with excuses about not enough time for the Word. I've already tried them all. They didn't work out. There is enough time in every day for God. Seriously, we're talking about thirty minutes a day. I waste twice that much on my reality-TV fix.

Does this require sacrifices sometimes? Of course. Maybe you'll sacrifice half an hour of sleep in the morning preshower, postcoffee. Maybe one TV show will bite the dust each night.

Maybe you'll set aside your lunchtime each day. You can call it "Scripture and a Sandwich."

Begin this purely as a discipline and know that one productive month in the Word will change you. What might feel contrived at first will turn into a section of your day you wouldn't dream of leaving out. You're going to have to take my word on this even if you've attempted consistency before and fallen off the wagon. Your interaction with Scripture will change your commitment to it.

Thirty days and you'll be a believer.

Safety in Numbers

When my oldest son, Gavin, was just shy of his first birthday, I scheduled his one-year checkup. I mentioned to my Girlfriend Jenny that we were off to see the doctor in a few days. She put her hands on her hips and asked if Gavin was off the bottle. He wasn't, of course, as I'd shrewdly discerned that bottle equals peace. She proceeded with a mini-lecture about how much trouble I was going to be in if he wasn't bottle broken. She said the doctor would get me.

I didn't really know what that meant. Would I be reported to the panel that writes books and tells us how to parent? Would the doctor quit giving me free antibiotics and wet wipes? Either way, I was scared. I spent the next week obsessing over yanking Gavin's bottle privileges and one long day holding a screaming baby after throwing two hundred dollars' worth of bottle supplies into the garbage.

I triumphantly marched into the doctor's office a few days later holding my sippy-cup-toting baby and awaiting an outpouring of embarrassing—but deserved—praise. Quite frankly, the reaction was underwhelming, but I did walk away with free wet wipes, so my membership in the Good Mom Club was salvaged.

Here's the point: The only reason I accomplished this step in the baby timeline was because I knew I was going to be asked about it. Otherwise, Gavin would have headed off to kindergarten with a bottle tucked inside his Spiderman lunch box.

At the risk of sounding too dramatic (which has never stopped me a day in my life), I cannot overemphasize the importance of accountability. My Girlfriend Trina is sick of the word *accountability* and thinks it's a cheesy catchphrase that has found a sacred place in churchy lingo. She's probably right, so let me explain. One of the most practical resources you can enlist in your Bible study life is another believer or small group of believers you will answer to every week.

Solomon says, "Two are better than one because they have a good return for their labor. For if either of them falls, the one will lift up his companion. But woe to the one who falls when there is not another to lift him up. . . . And if one can overpower him who is alone, two can resist him. A cord of three strands is not quickly torn apart" (Ecclesiastes 4:9-10,12). So true. If you desire a good return on your labor in the Word, *two is better than one*.

We are a people of shifty commitments and sketchy work habits when left to our own devices. A friend not only sharpens our mind and contributes to the depth of our understanding, but she also looks us in the eye and asks, "Did you read? How much? What did you learn?" When we know we will answer to someone else, we are ten times more likely to stay in the Word.

Choose your friends wisely in this arena. Sometimes your closest friend is the same one who will validate your excuses and shrug off your intentions in exchange for an hour of fresh gossip. Better to ask someone you highly respect spiritually, not necessarily the newest candidate for Girls' Night Out. It is not productive to surround yourself with "yes women." You want someone to ask the hard questions and firmly hold the bar high in love.

Paul urges, "Be devoted to one another in brotherly love; give preference to one another in honor; *not lagging behind in diligence*, fervent in spirit, serving the Lord" (Romans 12:10-11). Commit to the same reading, agree to ask each other about time spent in the Word, share your insights and questions, and set that time aside as *sacred*. One hour per week of accountability will do wonders for keeping you on track.

In the back of this book, there is a study guide for individual and small-group use. It can be used in a structured ministry or simply for a group of women who plan to meet at Starbucks once a week. However you see fit to get started, prayerfully consider who you will ask to stand shoulder to shoulder with you in your journey through Scripture.

Let's sum up: God's Word *requires* interaction. My favorite tool for interacting with the Bible is structured reading with journaling, as it commits my attention and focuses my response. Structured reading includes the following:

- Deliberate, intentional reading
- Start-to-finish reading, whether an entire book or a character study
- Small chunks of Scripture per day

- New Testament: ten verses or so (Matthew–Acts can sustain more)
- Old Testament: follow subheadings within each chapter
- Slower reading for greater significance
- Consistent, extended time daily (begin with thirty minutes)
- Scheduled time for Bible study
- Focused journaling
- Weekly meeting with like-minded partner or small group

Are there other ways to approach the Bible? My stars, yes. God does not box the unfolding of His Word into a package and stamp it with a one-size-fits-all sticker. I am not suggesting that this is the only way to study Scripture and that anything else is blasphemy. And to be sure, there should always be a degree of flexibility when we travel the Word, as the Holy Spirit may guide us elsewhere in the midst of a book or story. But for me, carrying forward intentionally affords me the margins I need for success.

This is simply the approach that allowed a derailed, frustrated believer to fall in love with Scripture. Within a few deliberate boundaries, the Bible became the tool that launched me into a deeper relationship with the Lord. God has confirmed for me that our best conversations will always begin and end in His Word. It has become the cycle of communication. The cycle of transformation.

For God is not a God of disorder but of peace.
(1 Corinthians 14:33, NIV)

Part Two

Introduction

As we move on to exactly what you'll put in your journal, let me begin with some annoying things you do *not* have to do. You do not have to begin every entry with "Dear Diary." You do not have to write cutesy, drippy, sugary things (but you can if you're a dripper). You do not have to use complete sentences if you don't feel like it. You certainly don't have to write as if your journal is going on display in your church lobby as soon as you fill it up.

This is a place to ponder the things of God. It's a place to ask questions and celebrate answers. It's a place where Scripture is applied to personal pain and victories. It's a place for prayers. Feel free to ramble. Help yourself to a rant now and then. Feel like using bullet points? Fine. Written responses to God's Word can take the shape of every emotion, every season of life, and every personality.

Each chapter in this section will outline various angles to journal through the Bible. Not every strategy will work for every passage. Sometimes you'll write in an academic manner, and other times your response will be personal. God's Word will move you in all kinds of ways, and your journaling will vary from day to day. That's good. It should.

I encourage you to try all of the suggestions at one point or another. The more opportunities you give the Holy Spirit to enrich His Word, the deeper He can draw you into maturity. The Girlfriends who have gone before you through this endeavor say it took about three weeks to hit their stride, but from that point on, their connection with the Word was forever changed.

In these chapters, I have included excerpts from my own journals. They are exactly as I wrote them. I even put in the underlines I am famous for. Each entry demonstrates the strategy suggested simply to show what it might look like on paper.

Keep in mind that we all write in a unique way. There is no right or wrong way to journal through the Bible. Some ramble for eight pages a day, and some max out at two-thirds of a page. My Bible Study Friend Christina writes in the teensiest writing ever—two lines of writing per notebook line—so she won't go through journals so fast. I take one look at her journal page and break out into a migraine.

Your personal journals absolutely do not have to take on the tone of any you read here. Psalm 139:13-14 says,

> For You formed *my* inward parts;
> You wove *me* in *my* mother's womb.
> I will give thanks to You, for *I* am fearfully and
>   wonderfully made.

Those inward parts include your mind, your personality, and your spirit. You were formed to respond to God in the way that you do. Write the same way you talk every day. Just be you, girl.

Keep this in mind: Every one of us has dry entries. Not every single day will be bursting with insight and wisdom. Give yourself a break. Some days are breakthroughs, and some are simple responses. The point is to stay in the Word with a fully engaged mind and allow the Holy Spirit to carry you along. Now on to journaling . . .

CHAPTER 5

The Forest and the Trees

Grasping the Main Idea and Inspecting the Details

When I began teaching, I somehow made it past those precarious days of classroom prep and carried forward professionally in such a way that my students learned things and maybe got smarter and even advanced to the next grade. I had a blissful team of two other teachers, and together we shared three classrooms of fourth graders.

I taught social studies and science for all three, and I was the hero because everyone is good at those subjects at age nine. Because of the nature of my topics, the kids with special needs were included.

One of my favorite students ever was Ben. He had several physical and learning delays, but oh, that boy. Anyone who came into contact with Ben adored him. He was super tiny with light brown skin and this enormously curly Afro that stood up four inches (really) off his head in every direction.

Behind his thick glasses, Ben's brown eyes were the size of small oranges. His huge feet matched his huge hair, and he waddled like a cute little penguin possibly pumped up on meds. He never stopped talking and laughing, and he was our star.

My classes thrived on discussion. We talked about the world and current events and nature. With fourth graders, this was a double-edged sword. No one can chase a rabbit like a bunch of nine-year-olds (except maybe women). By far, the largest rabbit chaser was Ben. He'd raise his little hand and launch into one dissertation or another about dogs or bugs or Africa or cheese pizza (it didn't have to be relevant). The stories would build and morph into something grandiose, and everyone listened, of course, because Ben was hilarious.

However, as I had only two hours a day to create prodigies, I'd eventually have to take Ben by the face and ask, "Baby, what's the point?" His answer was to squeeze me around the waist and declare his love for me, which worked every single time.

So What?

Let me make a strong suggestion for maximum productivity in the Word. Many journaling questions and study tools suggested in the remainder of this book focus largely on the details of Scripture. This is appropriate when it's time for a closer inspection, but we should *first* back up and ask of every passage, "What's the point?" God is certainly in the details, but He's also definitely in the main idea.

With every encounter in the Word, the healthiest approach is to read a section in its entirety first — no stops, no notes, no flipping around. Read for the big theme. God never intended the Bible to be a string of disconnected details. There is a point to every passage, and the details will always reinforce the primary truth. If you think a passage doesn't have a point, you have derailed somewhere and need to take another pass at interpretation with the help of the Spirit.

As we search out the intricacies of God's Word, we don't want to accidentally miss the forest for the trees. As my pastor so eloquently puts it, "So what?" At the end of the day, what is this saying? What is the take-home value? What is God's point? He is not trying to trick us with a bunch of hidden mysteries. The plain, obvious meaning of a passage is the plain, obvious meaning of a passage. With the main idea firmly in place, it is then appropriate to go back and pursue the details.

Identify the general topic and write it down. My Bible Study Friend Laura reads for the theme first and then makes a title out of it for the day. That's a great idea, and I can't believe I didn't take credit for it.

I ask at least one of the following questions nearly every day in journaling:

- Play this idea out to its conclusion. If you do what this passage says, what will your life look like? If you don't do what it says, what could happen?
- Write about the main idea of this passage rather than breaking it down verse by verse. What is the big picture here? What is God trying to say?
- What does God want you to walk away with more than anything else today?
- What is the ironclad truth of this passage? Does the world see this as truth?

- How does this verse fit into the context of this passage or chapter?

Stretch It Out

From this place, the main idea can often be expanded through journaling. This is where the Holy Spirit can enlarge our comprehension and multiply His Word. Extending the main point stems from questions such as these:

- How is this truth manifested in today's churches? Families? Believers? World?
- What does this passage tell you about God? Who is He here? What part of His character is exhibited? What is His best name here (Comforter, Healer, Teacher, and so on)?
- Process through the main word or phrase that leaped off the page. Write as your mind works.
- Can you boil down a passage to cause/effect? (When we _____, then God will _____; or vice versa.)
- Write about any detail the Spirit helps you notice.

These are some of my favorite thoughts to journal. It's through these concepts that we realize just how relevant God's Word still is. His truth is always true. His Word will always apply to this twenty-first-century life we lead.

For me, the main idea in 1 Peter 5:1-7 seamlessly connects to our world. Peter was writing to the leaders of the early church. My husband is a leader of a church, along with thousands of other modern-day pastors. As I journaled, I considered these questions: What does God want me to walk away with more than anything else today? How is this truth manifested in today's churches? I wrote,

1 Peter 5:1-7: As the wife of a minister, I receive verses 6-7 with the <u>caution</u> that Peter intended: "Humble yourselves under the mighty hand of God, that He may exalt you at the proper time, casting all your anxiety on Him, because He cares for you." For us, two big sin issues often hinder ministry: 1.) pride, 2.) anxiety. I guess things haven't changed much.

Two perfect reasons are listed as to why we should reject pride and clothe ourselves with humility: 1.) We are under God's mighty hand. A little perspective ought to put me in my place. As God reminded Job in 38:4, "Where were you when I laid the foundation of the earth?" And 38:12-13, "Have you ever in your life commanded the morning, and caused the dawn to know its place, that it might take hold of the ends of the earth, and the wicked be shaken out of it?" <u>We</u> serve <u>God</u>. We are only called to leadership because <u>He</u> ordained it. What do I bring to God's table? Who on earth do I think I am? When pride rears up, I need to respond like Job did in 40:4, "I am insignificant; what can I reply to You? I lay my hand on my mouth."

2.) Humility compels God to exalt us in His timing. This is God's theme. Our payoff is exponentially greater than our sacrifice. Just like Jesus' <u>eternal</u> glory for His temporary suffering. God's rewards are so much greater than the satisfaction that comes from pride. Pride feels good now. It works temporarily. It deceives me into thinking that on my own, I just might be something after all. It invites and feeds off the praises of men.

Why does this approval draw me in time after time? Brandon and I know from experience that in ministry, this praise can come and it can certainly go. Sometimes in the same half hour. Its highs are wonderful, but its lows are more than devastating when our measure is the opinion of others.

Sometimes it just feels good to be thought of as good. But I know God is truthful when He says, "Pride goes before destruction, and a haughty spirit before stumbling" (Proverbs 16:18). I so want to choose obedience in humility knowing that one day, it really will feel good to be good because He has made me good. I want to be exalted by God — not myself.

When the praises of others begin to fill the places reserved for the approval of my Father, I hear Peter: "You are under the mighty hand of God. Check yourself." I've reread this particular passage many times when I've lost my bearings in ministry.

Inspect the Details

My dad is a master at telling stories. We had a nightly ritual in which he'd climb into bed with my sisters and me and retell the same stories we'd heard a thousand times. Some were true from his days of growing up: "Grandma's Ruined Ceiling and the Spankings That Followed." Some were psychotic versions of the classics: "The Electrocution of the Big Bad Wolf." Some were secrets we were supposed to go to the grave with: "Why Grandma Never Found Her Cats After They Slept On Dad's and Uncle Tom's Freshly Waxed Cars." We kept that secret until junior high when the burden could no longer be contained. Grandma had to be told.

Those bedtime stories are some of our favorite memories,

so I decided as a parent that I would be a fabulous storyteller for my kids just like my dad was for us. That resolution died rather quickly on the vine after I began telling stories to my daughter, Sydney. They went something like this:

"Once there was a little girl named Little Red Riding
  Hood. She lived . . ."
"Why was her name Little? That's an ugly name.
  Let's call her Crystal."
"Um, whatever, so Crystal's mother told her to take
  a basket of goodies to her grandma who was sick.
  So she . . ."
"What was in the basket? Cheetos?"
"Sure, Cheetos. Then . . ."
"The hard ones or the puffy ones? Maybe Grandma
  couldn't chew the hard ones."
"Okay, cheese puffs that she could just gum. So she
  put on her red cape and started walking. Soon
  she . . ."
"What's a cape? Is that like leggings? Red is for boys.
  Maybe it was pinkish red."
  Stifled sighing.
"Yes, Crystal wore pinkish red leggings and took
  cheese puffs to her grandma. The end. Daddy
  will be telling the story tomorrow night."

A developed plot would have taken us to 2:00 a.m. Sydney's stories were over before they really got started because of the endless barrage of questions that accompanied every detail. And believe me, she *never* missed a detail.

Now we read books at night while enforcing a family rule

we call "The Five Question Limit Law" (For instance, "I don't know who brushed Rapunzel's hair after bath time. She probably just sprayed on detangler. That's three questions."). Some family traditions just weren't meant to be carried on.

Rather than call my only daughter "annoying," I'm going to call her a "detail person." Generalities are not enough for her; she will always demand more. She is genuinely interested in the minutiae of every element. While at bedtime this becomes laborious, there is a great place for this type of questioning in Bible study.

It is the truly inquisitive mind that simply wants to know more. Fortunately we're in luck; we cannot annoy God with our questions. He's thrilled that we're asking. He told us in Jeremiah 33:3, "Call to Me and I will answer you, and I will tell you great and mighty things, which you do not know." God is in the details of His Word.

To search them out is to search Him out.

He wants us to wonder about every facet out of pure fascination for our First Love. He wants us to look into the Bible and say, "Tell me more. I am so interested in You." This is where the beauty of journaling comes in. It is you and the Holy Spirit patiently working through even the smallest details and recording your journey as you go.

His promise is clear in Jeremiah 29:13-14: "'You will seek Me and find Me when you search for Me with all your heart. I will be found by you,' declares the LORD." He will be found by me. He will be found by you. Are you searching with all of your heart? An all-my-heart lover of the Word learns to ask discerning questions of Scripture, not for the sake of meaningless knowledge but for the express purpose of finding God.

Many journaling strategies we'll discuss later require us

to consider the who, what, when, and where of God's Word, but sometimes we need to ask why. As you inspect the details of a passage, ask the Holy Spirit these questions:

- Why was this particular word used?
- Why was it written in this specific order?
- Why was this included?
- Why is this necessary?
- Why was it worded this way?
- What is the response God is hoping for?
- Who is this passage talking about?
- Why does this part come before that part?
- Why do I need to know this?

We needn't be afraid to ask why about any Scripture. Our question can be wrapped in doubt or confusion. It can just be a question to which we have no answer. When we ask why of a perfect God, there will always be a perfect answer.

Every time.

David asked hundreds of questions of God throughout his life, and he summed up God's responses like this in Psalm 118:5: "The LORD *answered me* and set me in a large place." Large places are wide and free. They are places to grow and explore and discover what is true. When we limit our understanding of Scripture to what we can comprehend on our own, we find ourselves in a very small place. It can feel boxed in, and we wonder if this is all there is.

Journaling through the Gospels has probably been my favorite time in the Word. There's no one like Jesus. When Jesus said, "For whoever wishes to save his life will lose it; but whoever loses his life for My sake will find it" (Matthew

16:25), the question, "Why was this word used?" immediately struck me. I journaled,

> Matthew 16:25: I heard for the first time today in this verse "whoever wishes." It occurs to me that Jesus wasn't just talking about people who were actively pursuing all the false things they thought would bring them life. Otherwise He would have said, "For whoever tries to save his life will lose it." He was also talking about the "wishing" of those things. That heart matter of desiring life on my own terms even if outwardly I appear to be on God's terms.
>
> There have been tons of seasons when every person who looked at my life would have concluded that I was surely surrendered to God's will, but I knew and God knew what was in my heart was different than that. I've often wished for things to be how I wanted them to be no matter what the exterior looked like. I've wished for less sacrifices. I've wished for more things. I've wished for treasures of this world.
>
> God, my prayer today is for You to take my wishes and sift them until all that remains is the desire to lose my life for the sake of Your Name. This is a strong prayer for me, because You know I'm a stubborn girl. I have very definite ideas and dreams, but I don't want to be Your child who holds on to her wishes and decides how You fit in. I really want my deepest wishes to begin and end with You, Jesus.

Jesus purposely used the word *wishes* in that passage. He told us from the beginning that outward sacrifices mean nothing to Him without a genuine heart. He wanted me to examine my sincerity, but without a thoughtful consideration of Jesus' words, God might not have been given the opportunity to refine that hidden part of my spirit.

It's Apples and Apples

When I was in eleventh grade, I took chemistry under pure duress. We learned about that elemental chart thing. Hydrogen and nitrogen and carbon and such. Little circles with connecting lines. And did I ever use it? Never. *I knew it.* Is there even one person on this earth who cares about that stuff? I'm getting indigestion just thinking about it.

Where was I going with this?

Oh, yes. The skin slide. After we learned the proper way to use the microscopes (as in "don't put boogers under the lens unless you'd like a few days of detention"), our teacher had us swab the skin on our cheeks and put the sample on a glass slide to inspect.

When I took a one-eyed look at my skin magnified one hundred times, I was amazed. It looked so different from the skin I looked at every day while monopolizing the bathroom and spackling on the blush (and teasing my bangs, but let's not go there). Why did it look so flaky? I thought my Wet 'n' Wild base was supposed to smooth that out. Goodness knows I had enough on. Enough to go with my blue mascara, anyway.

After the slide inspection, I pulled the mirror out of my purse to check myself out from afar. After all, it was the same skin. Thankfully, the flakes seemed to have disappeared. I pasted on one more coat of powder just to be sure.

That is honestly the only thing I remember from chemistry. I learned that my skin can look one way when magnified and another way when viewed from a distance, but *it's the same skin.* To truly understand its composition, I have to look at it both ways.

Sometimes we take a close, magnified view of God's Word. We ask why, and we search out the details. Through the Spirit, we learn to see truths that require a close inspection, and images emerge that we've never seen before, even if we've looked at them for years.

But first, we pull back and look at the big picture of a passage. We're less focused on the minute details and more in tune with how they form together. We look at Scripture in its entirety and say, "That's what it is about." The *details* make up the *whole*, and as we search the Word, we'll keep an eye to each, knowing that God inhabits them both.

I will bow down toward Your holy temple
And give thanks to Your name for Your lovingkind-
     ness and Your truth;
For You have magnified Your word according to all
     Your name. (Psalm 138:2)

CHAPTER 6

Tweezers, Velcro Rollers, and Other Tools for Girls

Bible Study Tools You Have to Know About

Our daughter, Sydney, pushes the envelope in multiple areas, but one thing she has always done by the book is sleep. She slept through the night at six weeks and never looked back. Don't fuss over her. Don't rock her. Don't annoy her in any way.

1. Put her down awake.
2. Cover her.
3. Walk out and shut the door.

When she was two, I was putting her to bed and decided to love on her with the stereotypical nighttime helps she had never required. It must have been one of those days when she hadn't worn her Halloween costume to Target or put all her shoes in the bath water "so they'd be more shiny."

I stroked her white hair and ran my fingers over her face. I told her why I loved her and kissed her fat cheeks and rubbed her back. I may have even sung a few bars of the "Sydney Beth song" of which I'll spare you the details. A couple of minutes into this display, Sydney looked up at me with her blue eyes and said, "Mommy?"

I sensed she was about to thank me for two years of wonderful mothering and declare me the most valuable person in her life. My heart flooded with warmth as I anticipated this precious moment with my baby girl. I smiled and answered, "What, sweetie?" She deadpanned for a second or two and said flatly, "Get out."

Nice.

No chance for the tender exchanges I'd always dreamed about. She categorically refused the nighttime helps. Just leave her alone in peace. She'd never used the helps before, so why start now? Because they're sweet and precious and the memories of them will get me through the teenage years when she's sassy and embarrassed because we listen to Guns N' Roses. Doesn't matter. No helps for her.

Most of us don't use our Bible helps either, but the right ones can make all the difference. They can save us time and improve the results. We have helps for cooking, parenting, plucking, salvaging our skin—you know, stuff we've got to do. Bible study is no different. Let me tell you about my favorite tools so you'll see how very simply they can fuel your journey.

Study Bibles

I'd first recommend getting a good study Bible if you don't already have one. How is it different from the basic Gideon prototype? A study Bible offers many helps within its pages to assist you. For instance, each page has footnotes that supply all kinds of information: historical or archeological background, translation clarification, definitions, or notes about the people mentioned. These are great helps and often fill in gaps that would otherwise remain empty.

Sometimes a footnote can spur us on to thought. James 1:1-4 begins with these words: "James, a bond-servant of God and of the Lord Jesus Christ." I found a footnote that read,

Bond-servant: Lit., slave, from a word that means "to bind." The believer who voluntarily takes the position of slave to Christ has no rights or will of his own. He does always and only the will of his Master. For His part, the Lord binds Himself to care for His servant (Deut. 15:12-18).[1]

This idea of being bound to each other grabbed my attention, and I considered it as I journaled that day:

James 1:1-4: The first thing that strikes me is James' greeting, "James, a bond-servant of God and of the Lord Jesus Christ." At this point, Jesus' fame had spread and thousands of Jews and Gentiles believed. There was much to be gained in credibility and even pride to be a literal member of Jesus' family. James (if he were me) could have easily identified himself as "James, brother of Jesus" and let the gasps follow, but he only identified himself as "a bond-servant of God and of the Lord Jesus Christ." Jesus had transcended the role of big brother to become Savior, and James' role had transformed from little brother to servant.

In fact, bond-servant literally means "slave" from a word that means "to bind." A believer voluntarily takes the position of slave to Jesus — giving up his pride, his rights, his will — to do the will of his Father. But to be bound is a two-way street, because as we bind ourselves to God, He binds Himself <u>to us</u> as our Redeemer, Protector, Refuge, Shield, Savior, and Father. We get a lot for a little, frankly.

Plus, God has always commanded masters to treat their slaves with kindness as He is the ultimate model of the Gracious Master. God knows that I <u>will</u> have a master. It's my nature. Calling me His slave is not a demeaning term. I will choose to serve something — money, power, the opinions of others, myself — so God beckons me to serve Him knowing what is best for me.

What about other masters? He tells us in Romans 6:9: ". . . Christ, having been raised from the dead, is never to die again; <u>death no longer is master</u> over Him." And in Romans 6:14: "For <u>sin shall not be master</u> over you, for you are not under law but <u>under grace</u>." Through Jesus, God has rejected many false masters on my behalf. My well-being is secure only in the merciful hands of God who binds Himself to every man who calls himself a servant.

1 Kings 8:23 says, "O Lord, the God of Israel, there is no God like You in heaven above or on earth beneath, keeping covenant and showing lovingkindness to Your <u>servants</u> who walk before You with all their heart." Just like James, I want to be bound to no one else.

For me, the original meaning of *bond-servant* transformed that term to become one of safety, not oppression and coercion as I'd previously considered it. That simple definition in the footnotes prepared the way for the Holy Spirit to lead me into truth.

Study Bibles have other features that can enhance your time in the Word. My Bible Study Friend Laurie used to say, "What is all that stuff? Does anyone actually read any of that?" There are introductions included at the beginning of each book that offer tons of relevant history in terms of the author, audience, time frame, and general themes. Many introductions include an outline of the book, so you get the main ideas at a glance. This is a valuable way to choose a book to study.

The back of a study Bible has some fabulous helps, too. There is a concordance with references for facts, people, places, and concepts that can assist you if you're hunting for something specific. Whether you need something on peace, parenting, or Peter, you'll find it there. There are often topical indexes that include more thorough references on major themes of the Bible such as contentment, discipleship, kindness, and other big truths of the Word.

I know it's tempting, but don't skip over the inset maps, timelines, diagrams, and charts. Valuable information has been organized and simplified for us so what we're studying will come into focus. Study Bibles have been compiled by hundreds of smart people who were probably in gifted-and-talented classes. Use their helps.

I want to talk about one more component of study Bibles that I categorize with Diet Dr Pepper and Old Navy (Things I Can't Live Without): cross-references. These are the small

Scripture references listed vertically down the sides or middle of each page. They usually have a small letter that corresponds to a verse near them. These are verses found elsewhere that reinforce a truth in the verse you are reading.

See, the entire Bible was inspired in unity. Solomon said, "The words of wise men are like goads, and masters of these collections are like well-driven nails; *they are given by one Shepherd*" (Ecclesiastes 12:11). The words of Scripture are goads to prod us and nails to anchor us, and every one of them was given by God. It stands to reason that when we need a little more information on a verse, somewhere else in the Word is an obvious place to start.

For instance, in 2 Peter 1:19-21, Peter wrote about Jesus' transfiguration and how it affected his faith and ours: "So we have the prophetic word [of Jesus' second coming] made more sure, to which you do well to pay attention as to a lamp shining in a dark place, until the day dawns and the morning star arises in your hearts" (verse 19).

In the margin, a cross-reference listed Luke 1:78 for the phrase *the day dawns* and Revelation 22:16 for *morning star*. I flipped to both places to see what Luke and John had to say about this dawning day and morning star I was studying about. My journal entry for that day read,

2 Peter 1:19-21: Given all that Peter personally witnessed during Jesus' life and the remainder of his own, the "prophetic word" of the second coming of Christ was made certain for him. Every prophecy Peter ever read in the O.T., with the exception of Jesus' return, he saw fulfilled in the person of Jesus firsthand. How certain is he that the one final prophecy will also come to pass? Positive.

so he writes to us that we can be positive, too. He says we would "do well to pay attention" to that prophecy "as to a lamp shining in a dark place, until the day dawns and the morning star arises in your hearts." There <u>will</u> be a day when Jesus will come back.

The first time He came, John the Baptist announced Him. When John was born, his father, Zacharias, was filled with the Holy Spirit and prophesied about John's purpose in Luke 1:76-79: "You will go on before the Lord to prepare His ways; to give to His people the knowledge of salvation by the forgiveness of their sins, because of the tender mercy of our God, with which the <u>sunrise</u> from on high will visit us, to **shine upon** those who sit in darkness and the shadow of death, to guide our feet into the way of peace."

The first time the sunrise came, He brought salvation into a dark world. The next time the "day dawns," He'll bring victory and there will never be darkness again. Jesus said of Himself in Rev. 22:16: "I, Jesus, have sent My angel to testify to you these things for the churches. I am the root and the descendant of David, the <u>bright morning star</u>." The sunrise already came once. Our shining light in this dark world is the promise that "the morning star will arise in our hearts" once again.

That Scripture in Peter was already beautiful, but when coupled with the other declarations of Jesus as our Sunrise, this passage became seared in my spirit. I've never watched a sunrise the same way since. It has become a promise to me—like a rainbow to Noah—that the Morning will always come for me whether after a long, earthly darkness or for eternity.

A word if I may: About once every three years, I decide to turn into a physical specimen of fitness. I join a gym and plan to work out until the sight of my sculpted biceps scares me. I psych up. I buy bottled water and soy products. I dust off my sports bra and head to Gold's.

Now, I know some stuff about working out. I've cycled through this enough times. Yet inevitably, I tackle every piece of equipment *on the first day* and top it off with an hour of "Body Pump" with some hard-bodied instructor who has willingly submitted her skills to the Devil for his use. The next day, I lie in bed trying to find a position where the act of breathing doesn't send me into gripping spasms, and I hate everybody and everything. My error is obvious, and evidently I never learn my lesson.

I overdo it.

A warning about cross-referencing: Don't overdo it. It should not be used to reference every word in every verse. Otherwise, you will quickly forget what the original verse was about while you flip around for hours. You'll be a Bible dolphin.

Be selective. Choose a word or phrase that carries significance either to the verse or to you. If you're studying eight verses that day, don't cross-reference something from every verse. And on a larger scale, don't try to use this tool every day. It's simply *one* option for studying Scripture. This should be an enrichment, not a distraction. Use this only to fuel your understanding of what you are studying.

I recommend spending an hour in the Bible aisle at a Christian bookstore if you don't already have a study Bible that you love. Look at all your options and pick one that fits you. Don't forget to check for print size, helps, cross-references, margin space, organization, and readability. I like each verse to start on a new line so I can find it easier, but I have issues. Study Bibles are available in all kinds of translations (which we'll discuss later).

Some have features galore, and others are more basic. My personal Bible weighs in at about eleven pounds, but I clearly need the help. And if you already have one but had no idea it was so chock-full of goodies, make a date with your Bible and become acquainted with all it has to offer you. Read those pages pre-Genesis and find out what you're missing, as there is typically a user-friendly introduction. Flip through the features and pinkie swear with them that you plan to stop ignoring them and will henceforth give them the attention they deserve and begin appreciating them for their unconditional availability and good intentions.

Version Immersion

One of the first times I was asked to speak in front of a large crowd, I suffered through some hand wringing before I committed. All I could envision was standing up there either contracting a spontaneous case of irritable bowel syndrome or throwing up on the podium.

The chairman of the event finally contacted me to see if I was confused or simply a rude person who didn't return phone calls. While trying to balance "confident woman" with "basket case," I told her I was feeling a tiny bit nauseous about actually speaking at this engagement, and would she prefer that I ran the registration table?

She encouraged me about the opportunity to touch the lives of not only believers but also a host of nonbelievers who'd be at this event. "What an opportunity, Jen! God has chosen you to deliver His Word!"

Okay. So there's that.

With her words ringing in my ears, I called someone who would shoot me straight: my mom. I explained my reservations and asked her opinion, and I'll never forget what she told me: "Honey, listen to me. You remember that every time you are blessed with the chance to speak in front of a large crowd, you have the privilege and the opportunity . . . to buy new clothes. Good ones. And new shoes." And I wondered for the thousandth time, *Will I ever be as wise as Mom?*

I called the chairman and told her I'd speak. Then I went shopping. She and my mom were essentially telling me the same thing, but one took the high road and one took the retail road. I needed to hear the facts laid out in a slightly different (superficial, if you prefer) manner.

Sometimes in the Word, we need to hear things a little differently for the pieces to come together—the same message with a slightly distinct delivery. That's why another study tool I sometimes use is reading a verse in a different version of the Bible.

Various styles of writing work for various readers. These versions have been compiled by godly people who want to put God's Word into as many hands as possible. Find what works best for *you*.

There is a wide spectrum of translations. The chart on the next page illustrates this.[2]

On one end are the word-for-word translations that use the closest possible wording to the original texts. These include the *New American Standard Bible* (NASB) and the *New King James Version* (NKJV). They sound more formal

The Translation Spectrum

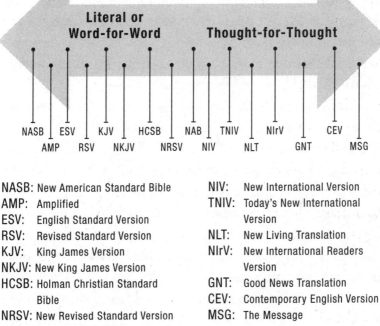

Literal or Word-for-Word

Thought-for-Thought

NASB | ESV | KJV | HCSB | NAB | TNIV | NIrV | CEV
AMP | RSV | NKJV | NRSV | NIV | NLT | GNT | MSG

NASB: New American Standard Bible
AMP: Amplified
ESV: English Standard Version
RSV: Revised Standard Version
KJV: King James Version
NKJV: New King James Version
HCSB: Holman Christian Standard Bible
NRSV: New Revised Standard Version
NAB: New American Bible

NIV: New International Version
TNIV: Today's New International Version
NLT: New Living Translation
NIrV: New International Readers Version
GNT: Good News Translation
CEV: Contemporary English Version
MSG: The Message

and try to render an English word for each word in the original language. They follow the original language's word order even when modern English might more naturally use a different order.

On the other end are thought-for-thought paraphrases. These emphasize simplicity and clarity and aim to translate each original concept into modern terminology. Some sacrifice accuracy more than others. I don't recommend them for your main study Bible, but they are often useful as a second

Bible. They show what one experienced Bible student thinks a verse or passage means.

In the middle are versions that are sometimes word-for-word and sometimes thought-for-thought, depending on what the translators think the context calls for. Examples include the *New Living Translation* (NLT) and the *New International Version* (NIV). You can see from the chart that versions lie all along the spectrum, as neither of these categories is rigid.

Word-for-word translations put more of the work of interpretation into your hands. For example, the NASB and the *King James Version* (KJV) render the Greek word *sarx* in Galatians 5:24 as "flesh." That's a literal translation, and you get to figure out what *flesh* means in this context. The NIV and NLT render this word as "sinful nature." *The Message* (MSG) offers even more interpretation: "everything connected with getting our own way and mindlessly responding to what everyone else calls necessities."

I use the NASB. I teach out of it and thereby cause weeping and gnashing of teeth for the majority of NIV listeners. Sorry. It's just that it's my favorite version, and I can't betray it. It's been good to me. We have a lot of history together.

Having said that, I know the NASB is literal and the wording occasionally sounds awkward, so I often read verses in a thought-for-thought version to hear a different phrasing, freshen up a familiar passage, or gain clarity.

So do I have twenty-five Bibles on my desk? Do you think I could manage those? I think by now you know me better than that. My tool is the Internet. There are several Christian sites that contain the entire Bible in many versions. I use www.biblegateway.com or http://bible.crosswalk.com.

There is an obvious place to type in the passage you're studying and the version you'd like to read it in.

Simple as that.

If you don't have a computer or have an unhealthy fear of cyberspace, there are other options. My Bible Study Friend Christi found a Bible with four versions listed side by side on every page. A quick glance gives you four takes on the same Scripture. It weighs more than her new baby, but it's awesome.

If you have a weak back, choose one or two translations and buy inexpensive paperback editions. If you prefer a word-for-word translation for daily use, try a more modern version such as the NLT for extension work. If you love the NIV, you may select a version on either end of the spectrum, as the NIV falls directly in the middle.

Do a little homework. Start by reading excerpts from the translations online. You'll get an idea of what each sounds like to determine which alternate versions (and primary version if you're also making that choice) you'd like to use. A helpful site I've found is http://www.zondervanbibles.com/translations.htm. The translations are briefly discussed in an objective manner, and an excerpt from each one is given. Plus, there is a graphic that shows the sliding scale of versions from the farthest left to the farthest right.

Remember that a translation is different than a paraphrase. There are several books out that do not *translate* the Bible but paraphrase the intent of each verse according to the author's interpretation. While these are great for extending, they do not hold fast to the originally inspired wording. They cast fresh perspective on Scripture but are best used as an enrichment tool rather than your daily version. As Rob

Lacey wrote about his paraphrase *The Word on the Street*, "Purist Alert: No way is this the Proper Bible. It's a trailer for, an intro to, an overview of the Bible (capital B) for those who've never read it, and those who've read it so much it's gone stale on them."[3]

Dictionaries and Thesauruses

Sometimes journaling can get a boost from a couple of old standbys. Just in case your study Bible and alternative versions start getting inflated egos, level the playing field of your bookshelf with a plain old dictionary and thesaurus. You probably already have a dictionary to prove that *quadrumvirate* is a real word you learned in freshman psychology during Scrabble matches.

Again, if you're into saving space, go to the Internet. There are tons of online dictionaries and thesauruses. Try www.dictionary.com or www.onelook.com for definitions. For synonyms, I recommend www.thesaurus.com or, for those of you who like word pictures, www.visualthesaurus.com, a subscription-based site.

These are the tools I reach for when I'm studying a verse I've read hundreds of times. Familiarity breeds contempt. It also breeds apathy, ignorance, and laziness. Taking a word from a well-read passage and freshening it up with a definition or list of synonyms (or antonyms) can breathe new life into what has become commonplace.

For instance, a traveled passage is Philippians 4:6-7: "Be anxious for nothing, but in everything by prayer and supplication with thanksgiving let your requests be made known to God. And the peace of God, which surpasses all comprehen-

sion, will guard your hearts and your minds in Christ Jesus."
Thesaurus.com lists these synonyms for *guard*: "protect,
watch over, look out, defend, secure, shield."[4] My journal for
the day reads,

Philippians 4:6-7: Anxiety. My nemesis. Worries can creep into
the sunniest parts of my soul without warning. I've worried
about Brandon. I've worried about ministry. I've worried about
money, time, friends, responsibilities, life. Then my children
ushered in a level of anxiety that I didn't know existed. And
all this for a girl described as "laid back to a fault."

Anxiety is a unique companion to sensitivity, intuition,
and compassion that God purposely wired women up with.
While men wrestle with their own companion struggles to their
masculine makeup, anxiety is a battle nearly every woman
fights.

But as I read this scripture again, the question for me
is: What effect does anxiety have on my heart and my mind?
The first casualty of anxiety in my life is doubt. I doubt
my security. I doubt God's provision. I doubt God's sovereignty.
Worry paves the way for insecurity even though I know that
God has a minute-by-minute awareness of the number of hairs
on my head. I end up doubting the very ground below my feet
and the strength I've been given to stand on it.

The second casualty of anxiety for me is distraction. This
is the deadliest in my life. When I surrender to worry, my
mind is consumed. I totally lose my place when anxiety knocks.
I can chart the seasons of ineffectiveness in my life and they
are linked to unhealthy anxiety every time. My mind is
designed to either walk forward in faith or fall backwards in
worry. They cannot coexist.

God commands me to abandon anxiety through prayer in every circumstance. There is no qualifier. There's not a graded list of situations where some merit anxiety and others don't. Verse 6 says, "Be anxious for <u>nothing</u>." It feels too big. Too unattainable. I know I can pray, but what about all the residual anxiety? How can I reject those feelings while I'm waiting for answers? It's a battle <u>I</u> can't win, but God never sets me up for failure.

Verse 7 says, "and the peace of God, which surpasses all comprehension, will <u>guard</u> your hearts and your minds in Christ Jesus." There it is. God's peace will intervene as the only antidote to anxiety. How? It will <u>guard</u> the two battlegrounds of anxiety: my heart and my mind.

The thesaurus lists these words as alternatives to "guard": protect, watch over, look out, defend, secure, shield. I'm struck with the image of God as the fierce Warrior ready to battle every distracting worry and anxious thought. After I've done my part to earnestly pray and release my death grip on the circumstances that stir up anxiety, God's peace will protect my heart and mind with such force that what should cause doubt and distraction in my life will have no room for occupation.

Does this make sense? No. It "surpasses all comprehension." Anxiety is so pervasive that it has become part of my makeup. Yet God offers me an ironclad shield to worry: peace. He'll bring it and defend its rightful place in my heart and my mind. "The steadfast of mind <u>You will keep</u> in perfect peace, because he trusts in You" (Isaiah 26:3).

While I'd read that passage countless times before, the thesaurus helped me envision truth in a new context: God as my Warrior—the Defender of my peace and the Victor over my anxiety. Although I hold the responsibility of prayer, God valiantly defends the peace He intended for me.

Set Up Your Space

My sweet husband grew up on a horse ranch in western Colorado. I've heard plenty of stories about log splitting and breeding practices that I've blocked with the help of a counselor. As a result of this upbringing, his dream is to move to the country on "land," complete with fishing, four-wheeling, and granola-type living.

As he describes this perfect, private life, all I can muster out of my city-snobbery existence is, "Sounds inconvenient." Brandon stares at me for several long seconds, trying to figure out what's wrong with me. Doesn't work. He's forced to put yet another of my statements out to pasture, along with "Pink is the new black" and "I'm going to be on the news tonight talking about bird poop."

Convenience—I'm shamelessly all about it. When it comes to study tools, you should be, too. None of these helps are worth the paper they're printed on if they're not conveniently at your disposal when you need them. They can be assembled and organized in one intentional day with a visit to your local Christian bookstore and thirty minutes spent online bookmarking some new sites. To recap, here are the resources that will serve you well:

- A study Bible in the translation of your choice
  - Choose your favorite translation at http://www .zondervanbibles.com/translations.htm

- Various translations of the Bible
  - Online sites:
    - www.biblegateway.com
    - http://bible.crosswalk.com
  - Bible with several translations included
  - Inexpensive copies of two or three different translations
- Dictionary
  - Online sites:
    - www.dictionary.com
    - www.onelook.com
- Thesaurus
  - Online sites:
    - www.thesaurus.com
    - www.visualthesaurus.com

Designate a place for Bible study where you can keep your tools permanently. If they're not within reaching distance, you're not going to get up to find them.

Set up your space with everything you could possibly need. I have Girlfriends who use colored pens, stickers, highlighters, music, note cards, sticky notes, crayons (I kid you not). To each your own, girls. If you want it, put it in the space. My Bible Study Friend Leah uses an enormous basket for all her stuff. She's a colorer. Bottom line: Convenience reduces distraction.

If some of these tools are new to you, familiarize yourself with the format of each one. Pick your favorite websites and create bookmarks on your computer so they can be accessed with one click. Prepare *first* so you'll be ready to use any study tool that is appropriate and won't waste precious Bible study time navigating a website for the first time or trying to make sense of your study Bible.

Practically speaking, do I use all of these tools every day? Are you joking? As my Girlfriend Ann says, "You're not that organized." As if anyone thought I was. I'm presenting these resources in a concentrated format to expose you to your options, but in practice, they are simply used as enrichments to Bible study. Although you'll practice using one tool a day this week according to the study guide, you *will not* and *should not* use study tools every single day—and certainly not all of them in one day when you're on your own. Try that for a week or two and you'll have to check yourself into Bible Rehab.

If you use *only one tool once a week* for six months until you're comfortable, that is an absolute win. Maybe the first week, you use an alternative translation one day. Then the next week, you look in a thesaurus one day. On the remaining days, use various strategies from the other chapters. Over time, the Holy Spirit will teach you discernment, and you will instinctively learn which one to reach for. As you are learning, be encouraged that the Spirit never turns away the heart seeking His Word. We risk a few precarious feet with new methods and sincere motives, and the Spirit spans the length of the universe to meet us there.

Get your tools together. Get familiar with them. Get organized. Get after it.

The beginning of wisdom is: Acquire wisdom;
And with all your acquiring, get understanding.
Prize her, and she will exalt you;
She will honor you if you embrace her.

She will place on your head a garland of grace;
She will present you with a crown of beauty.
(Proverbs 4:7-9)

CHAPTER 7

It's Not Just for Nerds

How Understanding Relevant History Makes All the Difference

My husband was a pastor of student life for twelve years. I could ramble endlessly with stories about bus-ride traumas and butter-knife-in-the-water-balloon launches from the third story (you don't want to know). As a mom once asked me, "Why would you want to do that? I don't even like my own kids."

We obviously went into student ministry for the money, and it's a miracle anyone voluntarily works in it. I've heard it likened to the appeal of foreign missions, yet we had tons who wanted to plug in and help. Understanding that something had to be marginally wrong with student-ministry volunteers, Brandon implemented an extensive application process for potential workers. They could fess up to anything they wanted us to hear from them rather than elsewhere (like a rap sheet). In addition to a written testimony and question-naire, each applicant agreed to a background check.

This information proved invaluable. It was a founda-tion for choosing workers and identifying the best place for them to serve. We gained an accurate picture of the entire person—both past and present. Because of this process, we had a stellar group of workers who voluntarily submitted themselves to teenage ridicule, public humiliation, and sleep deprivation. Good people.

You cannot underestimate the importance of knowing a little history. Relevant background frames the present and helps you understand what you're dealing with. This is espe-cially true in Bible study. Hebrews 2:1 says this of God's Word: "We must *pay much closer attention* to what we have heard, so that we do not drift away from it."

Paying closer attention is a challenge. We are a people of the superficial. Paying much closer attention requires looking beyond the obvious. This is often a matter of learning to ask new questions. Every word of the Bible was penned within the framework of circumstances, so let's start with consider-ing relevant history.

Who Wrote It?

I love to read. I've watched many a 4:00 a.m. come and go while in the latter stages of a good book. My favorites are courtroom novels. I realize that fictional law is more intrigu-ing than its realistic counterpart, which is why I read fiction and passed on law school.

My interest in these books creates a curiosity about the authors. I love to read their bios or listen to interviews to learn about their lives. They talk about their crazy clients and backward towns and college years, and ultimately I feel as if I know them.

I become invested as I read their books, smiling knowingly as I recognize a character or a case the author once mentioned in an interview—as if he and I share some secret or I've been given the private scoop on his plot developments. I almost feel as though we're old friends—except we're totally not. Being delusional runs in my family.

Knowing about the author lends credibility to his writing, gives us context, and connects us intimately to what he wrote. This is why I spend time getting to know the author of a book of the Bible *before* I read it.

All sixty-six books were written by someone. These men were colorful, brave, passionate, and full of experiences that fueled their writing. Understanding who they were is imperative to understanding what they wrote. That is by design. God could have supernaturally written His entire Word down—as He did the Ten Commandments (see Exodus 31:18)—and handed it over, but He chose to use men. We can only assume this comes with purpose: There is something worth knowing about every chosen writer.

Cut to your handy study Bible. After you've chosen a book or story to study, spend a few days meeting the author before you read verse 1. Here are some questions I ask about the author before I read his book:

- What is the author's history and background?
  - What type of family did he come from?
  - Do we know anything about his childhood?
  - What was his profession?

- Where was he from?
- Who was he writing to? Why?
- What were some of his major life experiences?
- How had he been shaped? What was he like? Strong? Bold? Timid? Gentle?
- What was his faith like? What was his relationship with God like?
- Did he have a personal earthly relationship with Jesus? (if a New Testament writer)
  - What was it like?
- How did God first call him?
- Did he ever experience a turning point in his life?
- Who were his friends? Mentors? Closest people?

The Bible offers more information on some authors than others, but some answers just require a little digging. If you have a good study Bible, the introduction to each book will fill in some gaps about authorship and audience. That's a great starting place.

From there, learning to navigate your Bible will prove invaluable. In many cases, your concordance will list the author's name with multiple references. Jot them down and dig in. For each Scripture you look up, check out the cross-references to find other passages attached to the author's name. Look for additional helps in your study Bible, too, such as timelines, chronologies, or lists. Typically, the first few verses of a book establish important details as well. Explore those using cross-references and footnotes.

Take notes as you go, including each reference in case you want to look back, and you will soon compile an overview of his life. It's not necessary to evaluate every detail at this point. Just discover the general framework of his life.

Having this foundation in place will keep the book connected to the author as you read. You won't believe how often you'll refer to this information. His writing will be forever linked to his personal history.

Once you've done the background work and begun reading his book, you'll frequently process a passage through the filter of what you've learned. As you are reading, you may ask questions like these:

- How does this particular verse relate to the author's life or an experience he had?
- How does this verse pertain to something he wrote earlier? Is there a theme he was demonstrating?
- If applicable, how did his relationship with Jesus affect this passage? Was this something he heard Jesus teach? Did he witness this truth in some way?
- What is his writing style or manner of teaching? Intellectual? No-holds-barred? Tender? Authoritative? Knowing the author, does this make sense?
- How might he have felt? Put yourself in his shoes.

If you didn't catch the frequent references, my favorite disciple is Peter. I won't bore you with the hundreds of reasons why, but if you don't already have a favorite, let me save you some time: Peter's the man.

In his first book, he wrote about his friend Jesus: "Though you have not seen Him, you love Him, and though you do not see Him now, but believe in Him, you greatly rejoice with joy inexpressible and full of glory, obtaining as the outcome of your faith the salvation of your souls" (1:8-9). As I read that, I remembered a favorite moment from Peter's life that reinforced his words, and I wrote,

1 Peter 1:6-9: Peter writes with such authority now, but 30 years earlier, he was a different guy. He tells believers, ". . . though you have not seen Him, you love Him," from the Greek word "agape" signifying the deepest, most unconditional love which Peter was once confronted with.

I remember the week Peter came to understand this love. In Jesus' final week, Peter betrayed Him three times in His crisis. No question this was his darkest moment. He must have desperately wished to have those denials back, but the deepest regret was the irreparable damage to their relationship. Jesus was gone, and He left on the heels of Peter's betrayal. I can only imagine the tears he shed that week.

But there is no one like Jesus. After His resurrection, the angel told the Marys in Mark 16:7, "But go, tell His disciples and Peter, 'He is going ahead of you to Galilee; there you will see Him, just as He told you.'" That scripture is precious, because Jesus was especially concerned about Peter. He wasn't angry or distant. He sent word, calling Peter by name as if to say, "I forgive you. I still love you. I'm coming to you."

I believe this message to Peter changed him. When he and the disciples were fishing a few days later, Jesus appeared like He said He would on the shores. John 21:7 says, "Therefore that disciple whom Jesus loved said to Peter, 'It is the Lord.' So when Simon Peter heard that it was the Lord, he put his outer garment on (for he was stripped for work), and threw himself into the sea."

Sweetest Peter. He couldn't get to Jesus fast enough. His betrayal was forgiven. The relationship he treasured was *restored. While the others rowed to shore, Peter fought through the water fully clothed to sit at the feet of Jesus, maybe just to wrap his arms around Him and sob. At that moment, he knew agape love. He sat under the gentle hands of forgiveness in spite of the worst betrayal. His faith was never the same.*

So when he writes thirty years later: " . . . though you have not seen Him, you <u>love</u> Him," it is from the deepest place. He has loved and been loved by his favorite Friend who bore the weight of his betrayal, died in his place, and met him on the shore. Friend forever.

It's not even right to read his books without knowing Peter. Every word has relevance to his extraordinary life. And Peter can just get in line because that is how the entire Bible works. God chose each man to write out of personal history that He orchestrated.

There are a few books with unknown authors. As much as I'd love to know what brilliant writer gave us Hebrews, sometimes the Bible remains silent on authorship. This is not an erroneous omission; God simply knew the content was valuable enough to stand alone. In those cases, let's be grateful for the anonymous servants who gave us one more opportunity to know our God. Or you can take the less biblical approach, like I do, and attribute all anonymous books to Peter. (That was a joke.)

Let's Actually Talk About Religion and Politics

This might not surprise you, but I've never made it through an entire State of the Union address. The entire spectacle is just too annoying. I laugh out loud when the brownnosers give standing ovations after every third sentence, while the jaded ones glue their butts to their chairs and pout. It's this ridiculous display of "yes" men and angry men. Just let the man talk, for Pete's sake. The speech probably took him eleven minutes in the bathroom mirror, but it takes an hour to get through it on air.

However, if you can get past the pomp and circumstance and listen, you'll be a more informed citizen than the rest of us who switched to *American Idol* halfway through. You'll hear that our economy is booming! Most of our graduates can read! The rest of the world likes us! (There is much exaggeration, obviously.) You can walk away from the address with a decent—if not inflated—idea of what has gone on in our country that year. Try not to get distracted by the standing ovations.

Often in Bible study, we need a "State of the Union." The condition of the world at the time of writing is wholly relevant to the content. Being aware of the divisions of countries, people in power, religious differences, and the hearts of the faithful makes the difference in understanding biblical truths.

For example, Israel was ruled by judges for 350 years until 1050 BC. Samuel was the last judge during one of the darkest periods of Israel's history, in which he constantly called the people to revival. He was also the first kingmaker. He first appointed Saul and next David. The point? This was the state of the world during 1 Samuel. The book chronicles the complete shift of power and allegiance that occurred as the nation transitioned from Samuel to Saul to David. This helps us understand the struggles of Israel within 1 Samuel.

Take a look at the New Testament: Paul wrote 1 Corinthians to the church he founded in Corinth, a port city and wealthy commercial center. It had an outdoor theater that accommodated twenty thousand people, athletic games eclipsed only by the Olympics, a multiethnic population, and the temple of Aphrodite, which hosted one thousand prostitutes. There were countless taverns and liquor lockers in the marketplace. Corinth was everything sinful. Paul began this church and stayed with it for eighteen months, but not surprisingly, it soon struggled with divisions and immorality. This prompted the writing of 1 Corinthians. Understanding the city and self-indulgent climate is imperative to reading this letter as it was intended.[1]

Do you see where I'm going with this? If we're serious about digging into God's Word, we have to be students of the Bible. Studying takes a little work. It doesn't require an innate level of biblical scholarship; it simply requires more time.

You might be thinking, *And how am I to get this information—Israel and judges and taverns and such? This probably all came out of some Special Teacher's Manual from the Secret Teacher's Stash.* Please. Every bit of that information came from the introductions to 1 Samuel and 1 Corinthians in my study Bible. I didn't add anything else. It took me ten minutes to compile. It's not rocket science.

At this point, I usually use one more tactic. There is some information that is simply not given in the Word. But we are fortunate to have many Bible resources at our fingertips to fill in gaps and help clarify context. Wonderful books give the basic history and time frame of every book of the Bible, including background on the author. I'm talking five to ten minutes of reading. "Oh, that's where Samaria is. Oh, that's how the synagogue worked. Oh, that's who Jeremiah was." It becomes so much clearer in a short amount of time.

Here are a few resources I like:

- Nick Page, *The MAP: Making the Bible Meaningful, Accessible, Practical* (Zondervan, 2002)
- John MacArthur, *The MacArthur Bible Handbook: The Ultimate Book-by-Book Survey of the Bible* (Nelson, 2003)
- James S. Bell Jr. and Stan Campbell, *The Complete Idiot's Guide to the Bible* (Alpha, 2002)
- www.bible-history.com (click on *search* and type the place or person you're studying)

There are certainly others, so check them out. You'll want one that clearly describes each book, including its author and context. This will add only a few minutes to your study time, but the payoff will be shocking.

It's simply deciding to know more.

In terms of historical significance, these are some questions I ask while reading Scripture:

- What was going on while this was written? In this city? In the country?
- Were there any issues the author was dealing with? Are they the same today? Are they issues you personally struggle with?
- Is a specific person named in this passage? Who was he, and what was his relationship to the author or character?
- What was the state of faith in the world at this time?

- Are there references to a place or event? What was the significance of it?
- Was Scripture quoted from elsewhere in the Bible? Why was it included?

I've always had a passion for the church. My husband and I are devoted to its advancement, so I read intentionally about its early beginnings. I'm aware that with people like me in leadership, there is a good chance I could screw things up. I may have already done that once or ninety times.

So as I read about the beginning of the New Testament church in Acts 2, I paid closer attention to the details of this wonderful day. Acts 2:1 begins by saying, "When the day of *Pentecost* had come, they were all together in one place." As this historical holiday popped up, I asked, *Are there references to a place or event? What was the significance of it?* My journal reads,

> Acts 2:1-2: My Bible has the heading: "Pentecost: Birthday of the Church." All of history has led up to this special day. Jesus has just risen and ascended to heaven. We stand clean before Him covered in the sacrifice of Jesus. All the groundwork has been laid, and it's time for God to begin His church.
>
> I know for sure that God is always deliberate. Nothing is random, so why did He choose Pentecost as the day to launch His church? Why not some other Jewish holiday? I don't even know them all, but there are a bunch. Why Pentecost? There has to be a reason.
>
> My cross-reference sent me to Leviticus 23 where it was first explained. It is distinct from all the other holidays, because the grain offering presented to God is made with

leaven. Offerings have to be made with <u>unleavened</u> bread every other day of the year.

Since the beginning, leaven has been a symbol of sin. Jesus said in Matthew 16:6, "Watch out and beware of the leaven of the Pharisees and Sadducees." 1 Cor. 5:6 says, "Do you not know that a little leaven leavens the whole lump of dough?" Leaven is bad, so why did God launch His church on the one day when the symbol of sin was acceptable?

It must be because God's church was always to be a sanctuary for sinners. He'd had enough of the gathering of the "righteous" . . . it was called the temple. This was His church. Sinners welcome.

Jesus told us the same thing in Matthew 9:12-13: "It is not those who are healthy who need a physician, but those who are sick. But go and learn what this means: 'I desire compassion, and not sacrifice,' for I did not come to call the righteous, but sinners."

<u>This</u> is the church that I love and the only one I'd ever be accepted in. This is who God is. He is, above all things — merciful. The purpose of His church is to be a place where the sinful and the lost can find the One Love that will never fail us. It was never intended to be a showcase of the "perfect." The righteous don't need Him; but Jesus has always been a "friend of sinners," and His church is our home.

God has always been consistent about what His church should look like. We distorted the vision, which led to condemnation. The significance of Pentecost was there all along; it just required nine or ten extra minutes of attention to discover it.

Who Are These People?

My Friend Andy tells the greatest stories about his colorful parents. Let me give you a visual: Every day they wear matching clothes that his *dad* sews—jogging suits, dancing outfits, jammies. Red silk. Purple satin. Think shimmering. They carry their own CD of karaoke tunes that they can hand to any DJ at any time. They travel in an RV and chain-smoke. Can you see them?

He told me they were once on *Texas Justice*, which is a small-town version of *The People's Court*. They were approached by the show's producers, who caught wind of their business dispute in the local paper. Among karaoke bars and their RV, they owned an exotic bird store (fits right in). A twelve-hundred-dollar African Grey apparently died three days after his wings were clipped at the store. Tragedy begat litigation. They rode to the courtroom in a limo. They wore maroon stripes. They lost. However, they were gussied up by a real makeup artist, so really everyone was a winner.

Talk about a couple of characters.

We remember characters, don't we? We think about them, tell stories about them, and like to spend time with them. It doesn't take a Harvard grad to figure out that God is infinitely creative—just look at us. There is a reason God included stories of His people in Scripture. He could have told us how to live in a few short books, but instead, the Bible is full of amazing people.

But are these characters people we can relate to? Their stories were relevant in the dust-and-sandal days, but everything is different now, right? I mean, our cell phones take pictures, and we drive Suburbans. We have our babies in hospitals (except my California friends), and how many professional tentmakers and fishermen do you know?

True. But we laugh, grieve, go to battle, move, change, sacrifice, and serve—just like God's characters. While the world looks different and many factors have changed, people are people. The same victories and struggles and personalities have always existed.

Solomon put it well in Ecclesiastes 1:9-10:

What has been will be again,
   what has been done will be done again;
   there is nothing new under the sun.
Is there anything of which one can say,
   "Look! This is something new"?
It was here already, long ago;
   it was here before our time. (NIV)

Called to something you're terrified of? Check out Jonah. You are woman; hear you roar? Read about Deborah in the seventh book of the Bible. Underdog? Listen to young David. You've been violated? So was Tamar. Struggle with staying faithful? See the entire history of Israel. A little impulsive? You'll love Peter. Girls, there is nothing new under the sun. God gave us the stories of His people because they're just like us.

Not only can we walk the journeys of our characters, but we also get to see how God deals with real people. He's always been the same. If all we ever read were "The Rules of God," we'd never understand how He has administered compassion from the beginning of time. We wouldn't know how He gave laughter back to Sarah or how He stood with

Shadrach, Meshach, and Abednego in the flames. We'd miss the moment He told young Jeremiah, "Before I formed you, I already knew you. Do not be afraid" (Jeremiah 1:5,8, paraphrased). This is the same God who said to Gideon, "I'll wait for you" (Judges 6:18, paraphrased). He counted Abraham's faith as righteousness to him, yet as Paul said in Romans 4:23-24, "The words 'it was credited to him' were written not for [Abraham] alone, but also *for us*, to whom God will credit righteousness—for us who believe in him who raised Jesus our Lord from the dead" (NIV).

Through God's stories, He tells us, "See? You can trust Me. This is how I love. This is who I am. I'm the same God to you, and you're safe with Me."

It's the Ultimate Résumé.

The love story of God doesn't begin in the Gospels. It began in the garden. The stories and characters in the Old Testament introduce us to a God who calls His people friends, beloved, children, redeemed. He has *always* said, "I will love you, protect you, forgive you, sustain you."

Many characters and stories are in the Old Testament but certainly not all of them; don't forget the Gospels and Acts. When I'm reading passages about people and places, I consult a special set of questions as I journal:

- How was this character called by God? Why him or her? What does this tell you about who God is?
- How would you characterize the relationship between the character and God?
- What was the conflict? How does this apply to modern times? To you?
- What does God require of this person or people?

Why? How does God require the same of you?

- What can you learn about obedience? Disobedience?
- .Did anything have to be sacrificed to fully follow God? How is this still true today?
- What can you learn from the exchanges and conversations between the character and God? How did they talk? What did they say? What was the tone?
- What can you learn from the earthly relationships (positive and negative) in this story? Do you have a comparable relationship in your life?
- What does God exhibit in this story? Faithfulness? Judgment? Mercy? Strength? What else? When has He extended that to you?
- How do you relate to this character? This conflict? This circumstance?

Now, I don't know how you feel about history in general. Maybe you love it. Maybe you think that those who don't know history are condemned to repeat it. Or maybe you lump history together with counting calories in the "Who Cares?" category. Whatever your thoughts are, if you decide to give history a little attention as you study the Word, the Bible will never be the same to you.

Will you be able to answer every question suggested in every study? No, but asking them will teach you to study Scripture from a new perspective. What may feel awkward initially will become a habit. You will soon discover—I promise this is true—that these questions will become automatic. You'll consult the question list less and less as you find yourself instinctively asking more of every passage. Once you learn to dive deeper into Scripture, you'll never go back.

This is how God intended for us to read His Word. We were never supposed to leave out half the details and read between the lines. He has offered us multifaceted characters with extraordinary experiences in a changing world—sound familiar? Let's begin reading it for all it's worth.

> For everything that was written in the past was written to teach us, so that through endurance and the encouragement of the Scriptures we might have hope. (Romans 15:4, NIV)

CHAPTER 8

It's All About Me

Discovering Your Amazing Personal Connection with Scripture

When Brandon and I were first married, we averaged seven dollars in our checking account. We were both students and somehow survived on our part-time salaries with a steady diet of ramen noodles and Little Debbie Star Crunch. I could often be heard screeching, "Turn that light off! That's ten cents an hour! *Ten cents!* You have *got* to stop with all this reckless spending!" Wow. I was fun.

So we were thrilled the day we received a letter that said, "Brandon Hatmaker, you (may) have already won ten million dollars!" Upon closer inspection, it appeared to be legitimate. Evidently, seven other people had already collected their share, and Brandon's name was listed eighth! It was typed and everything.

We were also informed that the contest was in its last

stages, and apparently we were in the final cut. We simply had to complete the form, mail it in (and a magazine subscription couldn't hurt our chances), and be home on Super Bowl Sunday so the Prize Patrol could find us with our five-foot check. The letter assured us that at this advanced level, there were only a few with winning potential as great as ours. Publishers Clearing House was thrilled to add Brandon Hatmaker to their list of millionaires; in fact, we were already considered part of the family. The entire letter was very touching.

We waited expectantly for them during the Super Bowl and even left a note on our door when we ran out for more salsa, yet in a shocking disappointment, they were a no-show. Great. We had preemptively bought salsa in anticipation of our millions. Who could afford that? We had only seven dollars in the bank.

Thanks a lot, PCH. Why don't you sound a little less personal? We shrewdly determined that the same exact letter was delivered to the masses—the *non*millionaired masses. It sounded personal, but it was actually a big, fat, stupid scam to get poor people to spend their money on a year's worth of *Reader's Digest*. Don't think we didn't cancel that subscription.

Let me tell you the best news: Although the Bible was written for all people, it was also written specifically for you. It is both a treasure for the masses and a treasure for every believer. God crafted His Word to lead you individually by the hand as you journey through life.

Yes, it is a corporate gift. The words in my Bible are the same as those in yours. He leads us collectively as His church and champions unity among believers through Scripture. But at the same time, it is a personal word from the Father to every believer. Psalm 119:105 says,

> Your word is a lamp to *my* feet
> And a light to *my* path.

What two paths are exactly the same? Our callings, spheres of influence, and journeys are as diverse as we are, but He has promised to lead us all. Through the Spirit, God can take His Word and zero in on an issue in your life He wants to deal with, a decision He needs to guide you through, or an act of obedience He is calling you to.

All at once, the Bible was written for *everyone* and every *one*. There aren't just a handful of lucky winners. John 1:12 says, "But as many as received Him, to them He gave the right to become children of God." Children of the King are *all* privileged heirs.

Here is what I know for sure: God is a God of the individual.

How does He speak to you and to the people closest to you? God communicates to each of us as one Father to one child. Your experience is different from millions of others, as God supremely knows how to reach you. He uses His Word to speak to you personally. Through it, He can walk you through decisions, call you to a task, and heal your soul.

The Daughter Clause

This is the appropriate place to mention the "daughter clause." I'm the oldest of four kids, and the top three are girls. My dad loved having daughters. Granted, my first Halloween costume was a baseball uniform that said DLP (Daddy's Little Pitcher), but wearing it was a small concession for the inevitable years of hairspray and drama I would later put him through.

Collectively, we girls came to understand that Dad would always be voted "Most Likely to Give Us Our Way." It was a black-and-white issue, so we went with it. We learned the art of subtle manipulation. We could craft any request to nearly guarantee the desired outcome.

Whether we played up his authority ("I thought I'd check with the boss of this house first."), manufactured a mostly untrue statement from Mom ("She said it was okay with her if it's okay with you."), or logged twenty minutes of snuggle time before the request ("Oh, hey, Dad? Do you think I could have twenty dollars?" said while under his arm on the couch), we secured a lot of yesses in our day.

Questionable means? Probably. But it swung both ways. Mom has said no to our brother only eight or nine times in his entire life. He lays his head in her lap, and the word *yes* pours out of her mouth and money flies out of her wallet. Manipulation is ugly—yet disturbingly effective.

The word of caution is this: The Bible can surely be a tool to lead us personally, but we must never manipulate God's Word to secure the answer we want. When we use Scripture to justify what we've already decided rather than to lead us in God's will, we are on dangerous ground.

Listen to God's words to Israel when they replaced His leadership with their own plans:

"Woe to the rebellious children," declares the LORD,
"Who execute a plan, but not Mine,
And make an alliance, but *not of My Spirit,*

In order to add sin to sin. . . .
For this is a rebellious people, false sons,
Sons who refuse to listen
To the instruction of the LORD." (Isaiah 30:1,9)

Ouch. Plans formed outside an alliance with the Spirit
are deceitful, rebellious, and destructive. Imagine how God
feels when we use His holy Word to justify them. He tells us,
"I am *against* the prophets who steal from one another words
supposedly from me. Yes . . . I am *against* the prophets who
wag their own tongues and yet declare, 'The LORD declares'"
(Jeremiah 23:30-31, NIV). Many have followed their self-
ish desires, attributed them to God, and made themselves
enemies of the Lord.

What are we to do? Many women worry about interpret-
ing Scripture according to their own agendas, not intentionally, but as people who have a hard time detaching from self-
ish motives. In Isaiah, God teaches us two things:

1. Do not, under any circumstances, carry out plans that
   aren't the Lord's.

And how do we know?

2. Form an alliance with the Spirit in the Word.

We form some unhealthy alliances, don't we? With
ungodly counsel, our own hearts, conventional wisdom,
worldly lures. These alliances have often determined "a way
which seems right to a man" (Proverbs 14:12) and used the
Bible to stamp it "appropriate."

As we encounter the Word for individual guidance, we *must* check our motives at the door through a healthy alliance with the Spirit. Jeremiah exercised wisdom when he prayed,

> O LORD of hosts, who judges righteously,
> *Who tries the feelings and the heart . . .*
> To You have I committed my cause.
>   (Jeremiah 11:20)

With submission, the Spirit will test our motives and lead us accordingly.

He will also test our feelings. Feelings are tricky because we feel them so strongly (pardon the redundancy). Many things feel right, but we must recognize this effective tool of the Enemy. He plays on our emotions not only because they are unstable but also because man has an unfortunate history of blindly following them. So the whispers come: "Doesn't this feel right to you? You can trust yourself. Your heart would never lead you in the wrong direction."

A sincere alliance with the Spirit will guard against this deception, but it must be a *daily union*. A one-time commitment doesn't necessarily protect us from the detours that seem so right. The Word must always be encountered with the Helper. It will become obvious when we have derailed because He is faithful to set up roadblocks in our spirit. It requires a strong team effort—hence the term *alliance*—because the Spirit can check our motives, but we alone can abandon them.

We must cross the threshold from faith to trust. Faith says, "I believe You can do it." Trust says, "I believe You can do it better than I can." It is at this point only that God can effectively use the Bible to guide us in decisions that we individually face.

Find Your Treasures

I saved these journaling suggestions for last because they come naturally. We have moved progressively from the most uncomfortable (Bible handbooks and such) to the place our heart leans on its own: the personal connection we find. As you journal, consider these questions:

- Did this passage raise a question for you? Write it down and explore it.
- Did you connect with this Scripture because of a specific life experience?
- Did this passage stir up conviction in your heart?
- What will these verses prompt you to do this week?
- Is this particularly meaningful to you for a reason?
- Does this Scripture mean something different to you now than perhaps it meant at an earlier time?
- Is God saying something specifically to you today?
- Is this true for you? Are you doing this? If not, why?
- Is this your struggle? Your victory? Your sin issue? Your passion? What truth can be found in this passage?

Allowing God's Word to speak directly to our hearts is an act of obedience. It gives Him the platform He needs to change us. As I read Psalm 37:23, I was reminded of a personal victory, and I journaled,

Psalm 37:23: "The steps of a man are established by the Lord, and He delights in his way." This verse sums up the victory over years of struggling. I've been a believer nearly my entire life, but for so long I could never believe I made God happy. The idea that He would delight in me was just too farfetched. I always felt like a disappointment. Even in the depths of ministry, I felt like my faults tainted my offerings.

Through the truth of His Word, God won me over and taught me to "stand in grace." I understand now that I make God happy. He enjoys me being me. He delights in me being silly or funny or enjoying my friends and family. Yes, I make Him happy when I use the gifts He's given me: happy that I'm functioning the way He created me to, and happy that I'm using them for Him. But He loves me because I'm His.

It's nothing I've done, it's just that I'm His very own child. He loves me because I am who I am. He can watch me and love me and be proud of me . . . and that truth is a credit to God who has given me victory over Satan's lies.

He delights in me the same way I delight in my own children — not that they are perfect or never let me down, but I love to listen to them play or watch them laugh or sleep. Sometimes I observe a quiet moment when they're not trying to please or amuse me, and I wonder how I could ever love them more. Nothing they can do will change that. I can't disconnect myself from the way I feel about them.

God delights in me just like that. Not just for the things I do for Him or only in moments of obedience but as a Father to His daughter . . . the object of His delight. Psalm 37:23 in the NLT says: "The steps of the godly are directed by the Lord. He delights in _every detail_ of their lives."

Talk about a personal connection. I'd struggled with that truth for years. Yes, that verse was written for all of us, but God took it and said to me, "Jennifer, I love *you*. I delight in *you*. I watch you when you're not paying attention, and I smile. You are My daughter, and I love everything about you." His Word was a lamp to my misguided feet to lead me back to the shelter of His delight.

Girls, if God's Word has been only for the world at large and not your personal love letter, there is more. Ask the Spirit to open your ears to the words intended for you and give Him the opportunity to lead you there. Claim the promises of God and allow Him to envelop you with His devotion. Relinquish your motives with the help of the Spirit and place your trust in the only One who loves you endlessly. God's truths will seep into the remote places of your soul until they become the air you breathe.

When my Bible Study Friend Christi wanted to express how precious the Word had become to her, she held up her Bible and proclaimed, "I love you so much!" David agreed in Psalm 119:

I shall delight in Your commandments,
Which I love.
And I shall lift up my hands to Your commandments,
Which I love. (verses 47-48)

O how I love Your law! (verse 97)

I love Your commandments
Above gold, yes, above fine gold. (verse 127)

Your word is very pure,
Therefore Your servant loves it. (verse 140)

Consider how I love Your precepts;
Revive me, O LORD, according to Your lovingkindness.
   (verse 159)

My soul keeps Your testimonies,
And I love them exceedingly. (verse 167)

This is the natural outcome of a life turned on end by the Word. It's the difference between receiving the Publishers Clearing House letter with the (correct) assumption that yours is no different from the one every other person received and discovering that you are the actual recipient of untold riches.

This is not a letter you pitch on the coffee table with intentions to get to it later. This is a letter that sends you screaming into the streets and hugging strangers. This letter will change your life and the generations who follow you. You'll come to understand that your days of poverty are over. This is the best letter you've ever read—and it's addressed to you.

The Lord says He gave this letter

To endow those who love me with wealth,
That I may fill their treasuries. (Proverbs 8:21)

The Bible is a wealth of blessings for every woman who would accept the credit in her account. It becomes your choice to live in extraordinary wealth of the Spirit, to subsist paycheck to paycheck, or to suffer in bankruptcy of the soul. The Word is here to coax us to the riches intended for us all along.

"We Need to Talk"

Years ago, my mom and two sisters were visiting us while my dad was on a mission trip. In the midst of this visit, it dawned on me that several weeks had passed without my attention, and maybe there was a reason I'd been feeling bizarre (meaning I had been eating such volumes of food that my husband was terrified). I could have found a pair of Steve Madden heels at Nordstrom marked for $7.99 and been less surprised than I was at discovering I was pregnant for the first time.

As my sisters and I jumped up and down and squealed like Girl Scouts, my mom sat there dumbfounded. I spent a few hours floating around in happiness, gaining weight by the minute, but my mom seemed reflective.

I finally asked her if she was okay, secretly terrified that the idea of me as a mother had her gripped in waves of panic, which would have been completely understandable. But she told me she just couldn't fully feel the joy until Dad knew. They'd been married twenty-eight years, I was their oldest daughter, and this was too big not to share. It wasn't until Mom watched me tell Dad on the phone the next day that tears began pouring down her cheeks. When she took the phone, she could barely talk.

I began to understand that in the most treasured relationships, some moments cannot be fully experienced until they are shared with each other. Even the greatest joys are incomplete until they are spoken to a soul mate.

Often in responding to Scripture, we write about history,

the meaning of a word, or a character. We write *about* the Word. But sometimes all that makes sense is to talk directly to the Author. To sit at His feet and pour out our hearts and allow His unfailing love to blanket our souls. We have a fancy church word for this type of engagement.

Prayer.

That's the ultimate goal, isn't it? At the end of the day, God wants all our efforts in the Word to lead us to Him. Otherwise it's just knowledge, which we are certainly called to pursue but only because the more we know *about* God, the more deeply we fall in love *with* Him. The greatest gifts from God surpass the place knowledge alone can take us. Paul expressed this idea several times in Scripture:

To know the *love of Christ* which surpasses
    knowledge (Ephesians 3:19)

The *peace of God*, which surpasses all
    comprehension (Philippians 4:7)

The man who thinks he knows something does not yet
    know as he ought to know. But the man who loves
    God is *known by God*. (1 Corinthians 8:2-3, NIV)

Love never fails; but if there . . . is knowledge, it
    will be done away. For we know in part and we
    prophesy in part; but when the perfect comes, the
    partial will be done away. (1 Corinthians 13:8-10)

In and of itself, knowledge is limited and partial. If knowledge does not lead us to the arms of our Savior, it is worthless.

This was the fatal flaw of the Pharisees. A healthy relationship with the Word will ultimately lead us to intimate conversations with God. Jesus spoke the truth about His people in John 10:27: "My sheep hear My voice, and *I know them*."

We've got to talk to Him.

The quickest way to add depth between any two parties is to constantly communicate. Sometimes that means talking. Sometimes that means listening. Always it means responding. Always it requires authenticity. A real relationship doesn't make superficial chitchat and let the important matters remain buried. It requires honesty and consistency. Without both components, communication will be hindered.

God wants to pull us deep into fellowship with Him — past knowledge, past understanding, past our humanity. Paul told Timothy, "I want the men in every place to pray, lifting up holy hands" (1 Timothy 2:8). For these reasons, we often journal with a prayer-based response:

- Does this Scripture answer or affect a prayer concern of yours in any way?
- Write out a prayer using some of the same words you read today.
- Write this passage as a prayer of thanksgiving, praise, or worship back to God.
- Rewrite this passage, making it personal to you (substitute your name, "I," or "me" where appropriate).
- Do you need to pray specifically for someone else based on the truths in the passage you read?
- What do you need to tell God about concerning this Scripture?

- What do you need to listen to God about concerning this Scripture?

Sometimes God's Word is so perfect that all we can do is say it back to Him. It so often expresses our pain, joy, confusion, or thanksgiving in such a clear fashion that our own words are inadequate. He gave us His Word to use when we don't have any words of our own.

Paul wrote 2 Thessalonians to encourage the church in Thessalonica. I read,

> We ought always to give thanks to God for you, brethren, as is only fitting, because your faith is greatly enlarged, and the love of each one of you toward one another grows ever greater; therefore, we ourselves speak proudly of you among the churches of God for your perseverance and faith in the midst of all your persecutions and afflictions which you endure. . . .
>
> To this end also we pray for you always, that our God will count you worthy of your calling, and fulfill every desire for goodness and the work of faith with power, so that the name of our Lord Jesus will be glorified in you, and you in Him, according to the grace of our God and the Lord Jesus Christ. (1:3-4,11-12)

This Scripture represented exactly what I wanted to say, so I borrowed God's Word and wrote it back to Him:

2 Thessalonians 1:1-12: Father, I pray that my life causes others to give thanks to You because of the faith You have instilled in me. Please enlarge that faith so greatly until You are all others can see in me. Increase my love for other believers until they feel touched by Your very hand. I always want to bring You honor and pride in my church through the perseverance You've developed in me. I never want to be the source of hypocrisy. Let the afflictions that fall on my shoulders be handled in such a way as to bring You glory, not sorrow. Be honored in my trials as the sustainer who carries me through. Lord, though it humbles me to even say it, please count me worthy of the calling You have laid on my life not because of my merits but because of Your grace. Find me trustworthy to carry out what You've asked me to do. Make me worthy in You, Jesus. My worth comes only from Your sacrifice. God, my desires for goodness are many, but they are only accomplished in You. On my own, I will let You down. Please fulfill what I long to do for You with the power, strength, and opportunities I need for obedience. My greatest desire for goodness in my life is that Your name, Jesus, will be glorified in me. Be glorified in me. Be so glorified in me. Be honored in me. Jesus, thank You for Your grace as You glorify me in Your name. Not in pride but as an example of Your love, Your goodness, and Your power. I will always glory in You.

How could I have improved on God's beautiful words? I didn't need to. They voiced my desires so clearly that it became an honor to pray them back to their Source.

Talk the Talk, Write the Talk

I was asked once, "Why should we write prayers down? Why can't we just say them?" It's a good question. The last thing I want to do is suggest strategies that are extraneous or superfluous (translation: an unnecessary pain in the rear end).

First, prayer is not defined by its means. Look at the

ways God speaks to us: through His Word, the Spirit, godly counsel, dreams, teachers, circumstances, creation. He uses any means necessary to reach His people. God uses some methods of speaking more frequently with certain children because He knows His sheep and He knows how they will hear His voice most clearly.

Inversely, we can pray back to God in various ways. Sometimes it's in the quiet of our kitchen before anyone else is awake. Sometimes it's in obedience. Sometimes it's driving down the highway, talking out loud while passing drivers assume we're mental. Sometimes it's within a choice we make. Sometimes it's when we write. This is why God felt comfortable telling us to "pray without ceasing" (1 Thessalonians 5:17). A prayer is acceptable to God not because of its format but because His child is uniting with His presence.

Second, our written prayers serve as a permanent reminder of where God has carried us. We are a people of the here and now. We quickly forget God's faithfulness. Written prayers allow us to look back at what we poured out to God—and what He poured back to us—and remember the One who is called Faithful and True. As Nehemiah said, "Remember the Lord who is great and awesome" (4:14). Writing down our prayers guarantees we won't forget.

If that's not enough, I turn again to the Word. I suppose if writing down prayers was unnecessary, we wouldn't have any in Scripture, right? Events and history would be written for us, but prayers would have gone undocumented because they need only be spoken.

If that was the case, we would have missed out on the moment of deliverance when Moses sang to God,

Who is like You among the gods, O LORD?
Who is like You, majestic in holiness,
Awesome in praises, working wonders? (Exodus 15:11)

How would we have known about Hannah's prayer after Samuel was born?

There is no one holy like the LORD,
Indeed, there is no one besides You,
Nor is there any rock like our God. (1 Samuel 2:2)

We would never have known Jeremiah's moment of insecurity under the weight of his calling when he prayed,

Alas, Lord GOD!
Behold, I do not know how to speak,
Because I am a youth. (Jeremiah 1:6)

Nearly every major character in the Bible records at least one prayer that was first spoken and later written.

Girls, what if Jesus' final prayer was not written down? We would never have known that in His greatest crisis, He prayed for *us*: "I do not ask on behalf of these alone, but for those also who believe in Me through their word; that they may all be one; even as You, Father, are in Me and I in You, that they also may be in Us, so that the world may believe that You sent Me" (John 17:20-21).

Writing down prayers from the depths of our souls is one more way to bring glory to the One who deserves it. It is evidence that every spoken word, every written word, and every thought within us will be offered as another opportunity for God's name to be exalted.

You Ready?

The Bible is not a subjective work. God knew at its conception how it would intersect your life and how it would intersect mine. He knew how it would lead you and teach me and change us all. It is the greatest testimony to His magnificence that God could craft His Word for the entire world and for every individual soul. And in our labor in the Word, all roads point back to God: in devotion, in obedience, and in awe.

Are you ready? Is the Word beckoning you to become immersed in its wonders? Are you drawn toward the only truth that will stand forever? And above all else, are you hungry to know the Lover of your soul on the deepest levels of intimacy through His Word?

It is your letter. It tells of the riches that await you. It will be the fire that refines you, the rod that leads you, and the hope that sustains you. Open your heart to the power of the Word and let God lead you into His presence. It is your soft place to fall until you see the Word face-to-face.

O send out Your light and Your truth, let them lead me;
Let them bring me to Your holy hill
And to Your dwelling places.
Then I will go to the altar of God,
To God my exceeding joy. (Psalm 43:3-4)

* * * * * * Afterword

Girls, I earnestly pray for you as your journey in the Word begins. Set up your study space with your tools and helps in order to minimize distractions. Check them off:

- Study Bible
- Journal
- Study tools
  - Bible handbook
  - Dictionary
  - Thesaurus
  - Alternate translations
- Computer (if you're down with that)
- Stuff you like
  - Pens, markers, highlighters, sticky notes, note cards, crayons, stickers, music, coffee

Decide where in the Word you will begin reading and ask a dedicated partner or group to join you in your efforts. Perhaps you'll be taking this journey as part of a small-group ministry. Whatever way you choose, decide on a time and place to meet weekly and make a blood pact (optional) that you'll be there.

A complete list of all the suggested questions and journaling strategies is compiled on pages 149–154. Tear it out and tape it in your Bible or tack it up where you study. Don't be overwhelmed with the many options. Pick one question and journal through it today. Tomorrow pick a different one. You'll find that most days, you'll make use of several questions within one journal entry. Be deliberate about journaling in ways that are outside your comfort zone.

You will find that over time you'll refer to the suggestions less often as your mind becomes trained in discernment. There will come a point when a strong, healthy interaction with Scripture becomes part of your fabric. Once the Spirit ushers you into the beautiful layers of the Word, you will never again be satisfied to simply glance at the surface.

God will receive your efforts and multiply them beyond measure. *He will.* I eagerly anticipate the breakthroughs, insights, and amazement that will certainly be yours as an obedient, all-my-heart seeker of truth.

Firmly reject any reservations or feelings of intimidation. Claim the promise God made to Daniel while he was seeking the deep truths of God: "Do not be afraid, Daniel, for from the first day that you set your heart on understanding this and on humbling yourself before your God, your words were heard, and I have come in response to your words" (Daniel 10:12). If you have set your heart on understanding God's perfect Word, He is on His way to you.

Keep this truth constantly in sight: God has given you His Word because it is *your* guide, *your* truth, and *your* hope. It keeps your head above water when the floods threaten to overwhelm you. It is the promise that even in the middle of a long, dark night, you never stand alone. It reminds you that even when the people you love most let you down, Jesus will forever be your rock. It is the avenue by which God holds your face between His gentle hands and says, "I couldn't love you more." It is the tool that leads you in strength. It is the promise of your inheritance and eternity with your Father. It is the rod by which God will often direct you back to safety from the danger of your wanderings. It is Jesus, perfect Savior and dearest Friend. It is your steadfast truth in a world of gray areas. It is your lifeline on this earth.

Through it, God wants to shower you with His love and goodness and compassion and hope. If God is worthy of your adoration, then, as Psalm 119:38 says, His Word is worthy of your devotion:

Establish Your word to Your servant,
As that which produces reverence for You.

Submit your heart to Him within the Word until your prayer becomes,

I rejoice at Your word,
As one who finds great spoil. (Psalm 119:162)

You are a child of the King. Through His Word, He wants to love you more than you can handle. He wants to bless you more than you can bear. He wants to lead you in ways that are incomprehensible. He wants to grant you understanding you are not worthy of possessing. He wants to uphold you when you have no other way to stand. He wants to give you glimpses of the glory He has reserved for you.

You are the blessed child of the King of glory, and He will carry you to completion. Submit your heart, mind, time, and devotion and allow the Father to transform your life through the beauty of His Word. You will never be the same.

My heart stands in awe of Your words. (Psalm 119:161)

* * * Journaling Strategies * * *

Establish the Main Idea
- Play this idea out to its conclusion. If you do what this passage says, what will your life look like? If you don't do what it says, what could happen?
- Write about the main idea of this passage rather than breaking it down verse by verse. What is the big picture here? What is God trying to say?
- What does God want you to walk away with more than anything else today?
- What is the ironclad truth of this passage? Does the world see this as truth?
- How does this verse fit into the context of this passage or chapter?

Extend the Theme
- How is this truth manifested in today's churches? Families? Believers? World?
- What does this passage tell you about God? Who is He here? What part of His character is exhibited? What is His best name here (Comforter, Healer, Teacher, and so on)?
- Process through the main word or phrase that leaped off the page. Write as your mind works.

- Can you boil down a passage to cause/effect? (When we _____, then God will _____; or vice versa.)
- Write about any detail the Spirit helps you notice.

Inspect the Details
- Why was this particular word used?
- Why was it written in this specific order?
- Why was this included?
- Why is this necessary?
- Why was it worded this way?
- What is the response God is hoping for?
- Who is this passage talking about?
- Why does this part come before that part?
- Why do I need to know this?

Use Study Tools
- A study Bible in the translation of your choice
  - Choose your favorite translation at http://www.zondervanbibles.com/translations.htm
- Various translations of the Bible
  - Online sites:
    - www.biblegateway.com
    - http://bible.crosswalk.com
  - Bible with several translations included
  - Inexpensive copies of two or three different translations
- Dictionary
  - Online sites:
    - www.dictionary.com
    - www.onelook.com
- Thesaurus

- Online sites:
  - ◆ ⬂www.thesaurus.com
  - ◆ ⬂www.visualthesaurus.com

Discover the Author

- What is the author's history and background?
  - What type of family did he come from?
  - Do we know anything about his childhood?
  - What was his profession?
  - Where was he from?
- Who was he writing to? Why?
- What were some of his major life experiences?
- How had he been shaped? What was he like? Strong? Bold? Timid? Gentle?
- What was his faith like? What was his relationship with God like?
- Did he have a personal earthly relationship with Jesus? (if a New Testament writer)
  - What was it like?
- How did God first call him?
- Did he ever experience a turning point in his life?
- Who were his friends? Mentors? Closest people?

Consider the Author

- How does this particular verse relate to the author's life or an experience he had?
- How does this verse pertain to something he wrote earlier? Is there a theme he was demonstrating?
- If applicable, how did his relationship with Jesus affect this passage? Was this something he heard Jesus teach? Did he witness this truth in some way?

- What is his writing style or manner of teaching? Intellectual? No-holds-barred? Tender? Authoritative? Knowing the author, does this make sense?
- How might he have felt? Put yourself in his shoes.

Dig In to Relevant History

- What was going on while this was written? In this city? In the country?
- Were there any issues the author was dealing with? Are they the same today? Are they issues you personally struggle with?
- Is a specific person named in this passage? Who was he, and what was his relationship to the author or main character?
- What was the state of faith in the world at this time?
- Are there references to a place or event? What was the significance of it?
- Was Scripture quoted from elsewhere in the Bible? Why was it included?
  - For information on the author, audience, and historical context, try a good Bible handbook:
    - Nick Page, *The MAP: Making the Bible Meaningful, Accessible, Practical* (Zondervan, 2002)
    - John MacArthur, *The MacArthur Bible Handbook: The Ultimate Book by-Book Survey of the Bible* (Nelson, 2003)
    - James S. Bell Jr. and Stan Campbell, *The Complete Idiot's Guide to the Bible* (Alpha, 2002)
    - www.bible-history.com (click on *search* and type the place or person you're studying)

Investigate the Characters

- How was this character called by God? Why him or her? What does this tell you about who God is?
- How would you characterize the relationship between the character and God?
- What was the conflict? How does this apply to modern times? To you?
- What does God require of this person or people? Why? How does God require the same of you?
- What can you learn about obedience? Disobedience?
- Did anything have to be sacrificed to fully follow God? How is this still true today?
- What can you learn from the exchanges and conversations between the character and God? How did they talk? What did they say? What was the tone?
- What can you learn from the earthly relationships (positive and negative) in this story? Do you have a comparable relationship in your life?
- What does God exhibit in this story? Faithfulness? Judgment? Mercy? Strength? What else? When has He extended that to you?
- How do you relate to this character? This conflict? This circumstance?

Explore the Personal Connection

- Did this passage raise a question for you? Write it down and explore it.
- Did you connect with this Scripture because of a specific life experience?
- Did this passage stir up conviction in your heart?
- What will these verses prompt you to do this week?

- Is this particularly meaningful to you for a reason?
- Does this Scripture mean something different to you now than perhaps it meant at an earlier time?
- Is God saying something specifically to you today?
- Is this true for you? Are you doing this? If not, why?
- Is this your struggle? Your victory? Your sin issue? Your passion? What truth can be found in this passage?

Engage in a Prayer-Based Response

- Does this Scripture answer or affect a prayer concern of yours in any way?
- Write out a prayer using some of the same words you read today.
- Write this passage as a prayer of thanksgiving, praise, or worship back to God.
- Rewrite this passage, making it personal to you (substitute your name, "I," or "me" where appropriate).
- Do you need to pray specifically for someone else based on the truths in the passage you read?
- What do you need to tell God about concerning this Scripture?
- What do you need to listen to God about concerning this Scripture?

Study Guide

As you plan ahead, notice that Weeks 2, 4, and 5 are divided into six days of study rather than five. In each case, Days 1 and 2 can be combined if you need to save time. Please be aware of the additional workload if you choose to merge them.

Week 1

Day 1: First, pray for the Spirit to be your special companion on this new journey through His Word. When I say "pray," I really mean it. Solomon reminded us,

> The LORD weighs the motives.
> Commit your works to the LORD
> And your plans will be established.
> (Proverbs 16:2-3)

Read chapter 1, "I'm Less Intimidated Reading *Shape* Magazine." Get in the habit of underlining, highlighting, or writing notes in the margin of this book as you go.

In your journal, consider the following questions and *thoroughly* explore your responses. Be honest and authentic.

1. Gloves off, how do you really feel about personal Bible study? Why?

2. Does fear play a role? If so, how? For instance, do your experiences play into any of these fears?
    a. Fear of lacking biblical knowledge
    b. Fear of failure
    c. Fear of getting stuck
    d. Fear of being changed
    e. Fear of commitment
3. In your journal, write about your experience of one or more of these fears.
4. What are your goals for personal Bible study?
    a. What current situations do you want to change?
    b. What do you want your life to look like as a result?
5. According to John 14:27, the world gives fear, but Jesus gives peace. We must recognize fear for what it is: an attack strategically placed to keep you from being *changed* by Scripture. Use Scripture to activate Jesus' peace for the following fears the Enemy uses against you. Look up at least one of the passages—one that is relevant to a fear *you* struggle with—and write in your journal how that passage can help you overcome fear.

What the World Gives	What Jesus Gives
Fear of lacking knowledge	Ephesians 3:17-19; Isaiah 30:19-21
Fear of failure	Daniel 10:12; Proverbs 16:3
Fear of getting stuck	Jeremiah 33:3; Exodus 15:13
Fear of being changed	Ezekiel 36:24-27; Proverbs 15:31-33
Fear of commitment	2 Chronicles 16:9; Psalm 86:11

6. Spend some quality time in prayer, laying all of this before God. Ask Him to lead you for the remainder of this study.

Day 2: Read chapter 2, "Nair, Diet Pills, and Other Things That Don't Work."

Spend a moment in prayer asking God to illuminate your Bible study roadblocks. Be honest with Him about your frustrations and ask Him for a clean attitude.

In your journal, respond to these questions and expand on them. Go past the simple answer, thoughtfully evaluating each one.

1. How would you describe your personal time in the Word right now?
   a. Extremely productive; life-changing
   b. Mediocre; sometimes interesting (when I read it)
   c. Frustrating, overwhelming, or confusing
   d. Nonexistent
   e. Other:
2. Why did you choose the description you did? Write about why it's mediocre, frustrating, or whatever answer you picked.
3. When you sit down with the Bible, what are your methods? What do you do? For instance, do you identify with any of the following methods? If so, how?
   a. Random approach (I open wherever, read whatever)
   b. Quick fix (a couple of minutes a day at best)
   c. Subject limits (I'll learn what I want)
   d. Easy road (I'll read what I already know)
   e. Dead fish (I read passively with no interaction)

     f. Marathon Christian book reader (It's almost Bible study, right?)

     g. Inconsistent chick (Is one out of seven days okay?)

4. How do your methods relate to your answers to questions 1 and 2 from yesterday? How do your methods influence your attitude toward studying Scripture?

5. Look up the following psalms, write the verses in your journal, and pray them out loud. Ask God to specifically illuminate any of your study methods that aren't productive—big or small. Ask Him what He'd like you to change.

   - 26:2-3
   - 119:66,173
   - 139:23-24

6. Talk honestly with God. Surrender any methods that aren't productive and ask Him to prepare your heart for change.

Day 3: Before you read, ask the Holy Spirit to talk to you today. Invite Him to speak your name and be ready to hear it.

Read chapter 3, "Codependency That Doesn't Require Therapy."

Process these questions in your journal. Answer thoroughly and honestly and give the Spirit enough time to lead you.

1. Where does your knowledge of who God is come from? How much comes from your own time with Him?

2. Do you feel as though your knowledge of Him has given you *everything* you need for godliness? What makes you say that?

3. What are your thoughts on the Holy Spirit? What are your perceptions of Him?

4. Who has the Spirit been to you up until now?
   a. A special guide through the Word; a Friend and Teacher
   b. The voice of conviction (which I sometimes ignore)
   c. Nobody; never really thought about Him
   d. Other:
5. Have you struggled with any of the following results of leaving the Spirit out of Bible study? If so, how? When?
   a. Felt alone, lost, confused
   b. Got nothing out of the Word
   c. Misinterpreted Scripture
   d. Had Scripture used against me in the form of doubt, confusion, or anger
6. Connect with the Holy Spirit in prayer. Promise to include Him intimately in the Word. Ask specifically for daily wisdom. Pray for godly discernment. He has always been your Companion, but commit to being His.

Day 4: Ask the Holy Spirit for clarity today.
Read chapter 4, "The Container-Store Theory."
In your journal, give an honest self-examination.
1. What is your interaction with the Bible like?
   a. I'm engaged. I ask questions and respond to what I read.
   b. I read and ask occasional questions in my head.
   c. I just read.
   d. Other:
2. Read Hebrews 5:12-14. How true is this passage for you? What stands out?

3. How do you honestly feel about journaling? What, if anything, keeps you from journaling?

4. Which, if any, of the following merits of journaling are the most convincing for you? Why?

   a. It forces my attention.

   b. It helps me retain what I read.

   c. It helps me process what I'm reading rather than taking the words merely at face value.

   d. It allows time for the Spirit to teach me.

   e. It's a way that I can follow the example of the writers of the Bible.

   f. It's my written legacy.

5. What strategies for structuring personal Bible study did you pick up from chapter 4?

6. Commit to a specific time and place to meet daily with God in His Word. Choose a time that is free from distractions and won't be undermined by other responsibilities. Pick a place that is quiet and conducive to learning (6:00 a.m., breakfast table? 7:30 a.m., back porch? 8:30 p.m., bathtub?). Write it down. Tell Him out loud. Be prepared to share it with your small group or partners in Bible study. Jot your meeting time down on a few note cards and place them strategically so you'll see them often. If it isn't scheduled, it won't happen (see Amos 3:3). *Promise God* that you will be there for the duration of this study. Every day. Same time. Same place. For the next four weeks, commit to your time slot as if it was the most important event on your daily calendar—because it is.

7. Write out the verse that gripped you today. Pray over it. Ask the Spirit to shine His light on the areas of

your Bible study life that need to change. Commit to obedience.

Day 5: Thank God for all He has shown you this week. Ask the Spirit to guide you tenderly through His Word today. Offer a new commitment to Scripture.

Turn to Psalm 119. Except for verses 1-3 and 115, this psalm is addressed to God. As you *skim* through this psalm (it's a doozy), compile two lists in your journal. While there are many options, look for seven to ten verses for each list (see questions 1 and 2) that *uniquely* represent your desires.

1. First, copy verses or even just phrases that *demonstrate your fresh commitment* to the Word. Pick verses that specifically match your feelings as they are *or* what you want them to be. Copy just your favorite few. For example, *tell God*:

   Your word I have treasured in my heart. (verse 11)

   Your testimonies also are my delight;
   They are my counselors. (verse 24)

2. Second, write down phrases that *ask for God's help* within His Word. Choose a few that are meaningful to you. For instance, *ask God*:

   Open my eyes, that I may behold
   Wonderful things from Your law. (verse 18)

   Make me understand the way of Your
   precepts. (verse 27)

3. Take your first list and pray it back to God in praise. Even if you don't have these attitudes yet, pray for them to develop in your spirit. You may say, "I have treasured many of Your words in my heart. I want Your Word to be my delight and my counselor."

4. Take your second list and pray it to the Holy Spirit. Claim His promises and ask for His supernatural leadership as you encounter the Word.

Week 2

I suggest taking six days for study this week. If you are short on time, you can combine Days 1 and 2.

Day 1: Pray for courage today as you encounter new ideas. Ask the Holy Spirit to show you truth and to give you insight today.

Read the introduction to part 2, as well as chapter 5, "The Forest and the Trees."

Day 2: You're going to practice identifying the main idea and exploring the details in a popular passage. Disengage from what you know and listen to your Teacher.

1. Read 1 Corinthians 13. Now stop. Let the Spirit lead your response. Listen to Him. What is He saying? What is He allowing you to see? Read it again if you need to and ask for discernment.

2. Now write about the main idea. Don't just fill in the blanks or write a five-word answer. Explore it. Write through it. Without pursuing details yet, respond to *one or two* of these questions:

   • What is the big picture here? What is God trying to say?

- What does God want you to walk away with more than anything else today?
- What is the ironclad truth of this passage? Does the world see this as truth?

3. Read over your journal response. Ask God to continue opening your eyes to His truth. Ask to be shown what the Spirit wants you to hear this week.

Day 3: Prepare your heart to hear the Holy Spirit. Tell Him you will slow down and listen. Ask Him to stretch you today. Reread your journal entry from yesterday.

1. With the main idea secured, let's practice extending the theme. Read 1 Corinthians 13 again and invite the Spirit to guide you as you respond to *one* of the following questions in your journal:
- How is this truth manifested in today's churches? Families? Believers? World?
- What does this passage tell you about God? Who is He here? What part of His character is exhibited? What is His best name here (Comforter, Healer, Teacher, and so on)?
- Process through the main word or phrase that leaped off the page. Write as your mind works.
- Write about any detail the Spirit helps you notice.

2. Thank the Spirit for teaching you. Ask Him to speak louder while you commit to listening harder. Pray through what you heard today and how it applies to your life.

Day 4: Pray for wisdom and a keen eye today. We'll be digging deeper.

1. Return to 1 Corinthians 13 and read your first two journal entries again. As you explore the details today, remember that they will always stand in agreement with the main idea.

2. Consider *one or two* of these questions as you journal on the details of this passage. Listen to the Spirit as He draws you to insight. Push through your limits. Let these questions simply be a starting point, not the end. You don't have to stay within these boundaries. Give the Helper enough time to show you more.

   • Why did verses 1-3 come before verses 4-7?
   • Why might Paul have used the examples of "a noisy gong" and "a clanging cymbal" in verse 1?
   • List the order of characteristics in verses 4-7. What do you see?
   • Why was verse 11 included?
   • The last phrases of verses 2 and 3 are "I am nothing" and "it profits me nothing." So what? Why was it worded this way? Where does this take your thoughts?
   • Why do you need to know this?
   • Why is this Scripture necessary?

3. Thank God for what He has shown you about love so far. Make any confessions or requests this passage has brought to mind.

Day 5: Talk to the Holy Spirit. Ask Him to meet you in the Word today.

   1. Let's test-drive these strategies on a different passage. Turn to Isaiah 45:8-12. Read all five verses and identify the main idea. Journal on this theme. As a

beginning point, consider *one or two* of the following questions and then allow the Spirit to extend your response:

- What is the big picture here? What is God trying to say?
- If you do what this passage says, what will your life look like? If you don't do what it says, what could happen?
- What does God want you to walk away with more than anything else today?
- What is the ironclad truth of this passage? Does the world see this as truth?

2. Ask the Spirit to continue to stretch you. Ask Him to show you any changes or sacrifices you need to make in order to hear Him more clearly.

Day 6: Have a discussion with the Helper. Thank Him for His leadership this week and ask His guidance in what has been a struggle. Join with Him in the Word today.

1. Look at the details of Isaiah 45:8-12 today. Read over your journal entry from yesterday and create a title out of the main idea. Now take a magnified look at the details. Disconnect your mind from cranking out an easy answer and listen instead to the Spirit. Ask *one or two* of the following questions as you journal:

- Why is verse 8 worded as it is ("down" and "up" twice each)? Is there significance there?
- What names does God call Himself in this passage? Why?
- What do you think about the imagery in verse 8? Why might God have given us such a word picture?

- Have you ever said to God, "What are you doing? You have no hands!"?
- What *should* clay be like? Why did God use this metaphor?
- Why is this passage necessary?
- Explore *any* detail that stands out to you.

Remember, open-ended journaling takes a while to adjust to. If it seemed forced this week, don't worry. It is a habit that takes developing. You're out of the box, though. Focus on what you *did* accomplish this week and spend some time thanking the Spirit for expanding your boundaries.

Week 3

Day 1: Ask the Holy Spirit to release you from your inhibitions today. Offer a willing mind to try new strategies.

Read chapter 6, "Tweezers, Velcro Rollers, and Other Tools for Girls." I will supply the study tools for you this week. By using my examples, you can become more informed about which tools you'd like to assemble when this week is over.

Day 2: Have a few moments with the Spirit. Ask Him to magnify your efforts, diminish your reservations, and lead you in strength.

During this week, we will practice using *one* study tool per day. Don't try to use more than one each day. In normal practice, study tools are best used sparingly. As I suggested earlier, when you're on your own, using *only one study tool once a week* is plenty until you're comfortable. Ultimately, you'll determine your favorite tools and use those more frequently. They should enrich your time—not distract from it.

For the next two days, we will take a look at study Bibles. If you already have one, spend some time with it this week. Read the introduction and look through its features. If not, consider getting one. You can find inexpensive paperback copies or used books online, and it will pay for itself over and over again in spiritual dividends.

1. Today we'll look at footnotes. I'll provide examples to use. Turn to Romans 12:9-21 and read all thirteen verses. Ask the Holy Spirit to stand over your shoulder. Identify the main idea and create a title based on it. Read the passage one more time.

The *NIV Study Bible* lists this footnote for verse 11:

spiritual fervor. Lit. "fervent in spirit." If "spirit" means "Holy Spirit" here the reference would be to the fervor the Holy Spirit provides.[1]

The *Ryrie Study Bible* lists this footnote for verse 11:

not lagging behind in diligence. Do not let your zeal slacken. *fervent in* = boiling with.[2]

The *Life Application Study Bible* lists this footnote for verse 13:

Christian hospitality differs from social entertaining. Entertaining focuses on the host—the home must be spotless; the food must be well prepared and abundant; the host must appear relaxed and good-natured. Hospitality, by contrast, focuses on the guests. Their needs—whether for a place to stay, nourishing food, a listening ear, or acceptance—are the primary concern. Hospitality can happen in a messy home. It can happen around a dinner table where the main dish is canned soup. It can even happen while the host and the guest are doing chores together. Don't hesitate to offer hospitality just because you are too tired, too busy, or not wealthy enough to entertain.[3]

2. Choose *one* of these footnotes and explore it in your journal today. Allow the footnote to be a starting point for your personal response. Detach yourself from a pat answer and let the Spirit expand your understanding.

Study Tip: Often as I journal, I ramble for a page or two, getting closer and closer to what the Spirit is leading me to, until *bam!* There it is. A treasure, one or two sentences that capture the insight of a passage in a profound way. I take my treasures and write them next to the Scripture *in the margins of my Bible* (gasp). Every time I turn to that passage, I remember what the Spirit taught me.

Day 3: Spend a few minutes with the Spirit. Ask Him to show you the unity of His Word today.

Turn back to Romans 12:9-21. Reread this passage.

1. Today let's look at cross-referencing. Pick *one or two*

cross-references from the following list or use your Bible's options if you prefer. Ask the Holy Spirit to reinforce the truth from Romans with its companion Scriptures. Listen closely to Him. Reinsert what He shows you in the cross-reference back into the original passage. Work it out as you write. Take the truth and extend it. Go past the "answer."

Original Phrase (NIV)	Cross-Reference
Romans 12:9 —"[sincere] love"	1 Timothy 1:5
Romans 12:10 —"honor"	Philippians 2:3
Romans 12:12 —"be joyful in hope"	Romans 5:1-2
Romans 12:13 —"practice hospitality"	Matthew 25:35
Romans 12:15 —"rejoice with those"	Hebrews 13:3
Romans 12:16 —"do not be conceited"	Psalm 131
Romans 12:17 —"in the eyes of everybody"	2 Corinthians 8:21
Romans 12:19 —"do not take revenge"	Proverbs 20:22
Romans 12:20 —"your enemy"	Luke 6:32-36

2. What did the Spirit teach you today? Ask Him to enlarge His truth within your heart. Allow His Word to seep in.

Day 4: Ask the Holy Spirit to open your eyes to the subtle things today. Invite Him to meet you in the Word.

1. Read Psalm 68:5-10. Establish the main idea and create a title out of it. Then read the passage again.

2. Today let's see what alternate versions can do for your time in the Word. Allow the Spirit to fill your mind with truth as you read the following translations of verse 6:

God makes a home for the lonely;
He leads out the prisoners into prosperity,
Only the rebellious dwell in a parched land. (NASB)

God sets the lonely in families,
    he leads forth the prisoners with singing;
        but the rebellious live in a sun-scorched land. (NIV)

God places the lonely in families;
    he sets the prisoners free and gives them joy.
        But for rebels, there is only famine and distress. (NLT)

God places lonely people in families. He leads prisoners out of prison into productive lives, but rebellious people must live in an unproductive land. (GOD'S WORD)

God makes homes for the homeless,
    leads prisoners to freedom,
        but leaves rebels to rot in hell. (MSG)

3. Guided by the Holy Spirit, reflect on these translations and journal about this verse. Whether you make lists, group phrases together, or simply respond to a

word or concept, allow the Spirit to bring you insight and lead you personally. Use this as a beginning and extend your response from there. Your thoughts do not have to stay within these boundaries. Where else does this take your mind?

Day 5: Have a conversation with your Helper, ask for insight, and turn back to Psalm 68:5-10.

1. Today you'll use a dictionary and thesaurus to enrich your understanding. Reread this passage and sum it up in one sentence.

2. Choose *one* definition from the following list (found on www.dictionary.com) and consider it as you journal today. Apply it to the verse and context of this passage. Let the Spirit broaden your insight. Slow down. Go beyond the obvious.

defender [of widows] (verse 5, NIV): 1. a person who cares for persons or property 2. a fighter who holds out against attack[4]

rebellious (verse 6): 1. resisting control or authority;[5] 2. prone to or participating in a rebellion;[6] [*rebel:* to refuse allegiance to and oppose by force an established government or ruling authority; to feel or express strong unwillingness[7]]

refreshed [your weary inheritance] (verse 9, NIV): 1. to revive . . . give new vigor or spirit to; 2. to give new freshness or brightness to; restore; 3. to fill up again; replenish[8] *settled [in it]* (verse 10, NIV): 1. to establish on a permanent basis; stabilize; 2. to discontinue moving and come to rest in one place[9]

3. Now pick one group of synonyms or antonyms (found on www.thesaurus.com) and apply it to this passage. What do you see? What is the Spirit showing you?

fatherless (verse 5): false, illegitimate, imperfect, impure, misbegotten [antonym: legitimate][10]

lonely (verse 6, NIV): abandoned, apart, comfortless, companionless, destitute, empty, isolated, outcast, rejected, unattended, uncherished[11]

parched (verse 6): barren, dehydrated, depleted, dry, fruitless, thirsty, unproductive, waste, withered [antonyms: fertile, fruitful, lush, rich][12]

[went out] before (verse 7, NIV): ahead, first, in anticipation, in front, leading, preceding[13]

inheritance (verse 9, NIV): blood, children, descendants, family, lineage, offspring, people[14]

4. Thank the Holy Spirit for a stretching week. Give attention to the insights He showed you and the tools that really worked for you. Your foundation is expanding.

   If you haven't done it yet, get your study space set up. Now that we've explored several study tools this week, decide which ones you want and get them assembled. Use a basket or bag or clear a shelf. Stock your space with everything you need for Bible study.

We will use study Bibles intensely next week as we dig in to history. If you don't have one yet, consider buying or borrowing one.

Week 4

This is another week with six days. Even God needed six days to create the world, but if you have only five days, you can cover two in one day.

Day 1: Pray for a passion for biblical history. The Spirit will give it to you if you'll ask.

Read chapter 7, "It's Not Just for Nerds." Pray at the close of this reading. Begin to surrender any negative opinions you have about learning in this way.

Day 2: Ask the Spirit to broaden your boundaries in a major way. Offer fully your time and attention to God today.

Let's check out how this works. Turn to the beginning of Nehemiah. Today we will ask these questions: What was going on in the world when this was written? What is the context of Nehemiah?

If your Bible includes an introduction to Nehemiah and other helps such as timelines, chronologies, maps, and outlines, use them to discover the state of Israel at the time of and leading up to this book. In your journal, compile the information you discover. You may copy it word for word, or you may piece it together and arrange it in order to best understand it. (Hint: For Nehemiah, most of your information will concern the years leading up to his book. Your helps will probably also point you to the introduction to Ezra as you establish context.)

This is also the perfect time to use a Bible handbook, where the information is already organized for you. If you're into cyberspace, go to www.bible-history.com and use the *search* icon to find out more. Type in *Nehemiah*.

Study Tip: While the Internet is truly a great source for Bible study, exercise caution. When you "google" a topic, every file out there will be pulled up, and many of them are completely erroneous. Some of the sites are so obnoxious that I would laugh out loud if I wasn't so horrified. Use good judgment and common sense. If the title of the site is "There Is No God," let's skip that one. Ask the Spirit to lead you accordingly.

Girls, do *not* get overwhelmed today. You need to reject that whisper. Think of this like any other type of research. Just because it's biblical doesn't make it harder. I once knew *nothing* about seizures. Then my daughter began having them, and I became an expert. How? Research. Diligence. Time. You can do this. Just dig it out. Look. Read. Flip around. Jot a few notes. Review what you found. You're not trying to write a dissertation. Just frame the context briefly with history. There you have it.

Study Tip: Do you have an extra Bible around? I usually open two different Bibles up to the same passage not just for the different translations but also for different helps. One may have a great timeline, and the other may offer more information about the author. Come on, it's just one more square foot of space.

If you don't have a study Bible or any other way to research biblical history (or you want to check your findings), I've included my own discoveries. However, *go at it by yourself first.* You'll be amazed what twenty minutes of attention will unfold for you. Find out how simple it is to dig in to history—and later this week, find out how vital that information is to understanding Scripture. Shut this book and give it a try.

Here is what I found to be vital information from my study Bible. It was already organized between Ezra and Nehemiah, and I excerpted what I wanted. Total time: 20 minutes.

Israel

Dates (BC)	
605–536	General period of captivity (Israelites taken from Jerusalem to Babylon by King Nebuchadnezzar)
605, 597	Leading Judean citizens deported to Babylon
586	Daniel and Ezekiel deported
539	Cyrus, king of Persia, conquered Babylon
538	Cyrus permitted the return of Israelites to Jerusalem (see Ezra 1:1-8)
536	Return of 49,897 Israelites from Babylon to Jerusalem
536	Altar rebuilt; sacrifice offered in seventh month
535	Temple rebuilding begun
535–520	Rebuilding stopped due to economic and political struggle

520	Ministry of Haggai
520-515	Ministry of Zechariah
515	Temple completed
464	Artaxerxes I became king of Persia (Nehemiah served under him)
458	Return of Ezra to Jerusalem
444-443	Nehemiah returned to Jerusalem
443	Nehemiah rebuilt the walls of Jerusalem

Nehemiah and Malachi were the last two Old Testament books written.

summary: Nehemiah completes the history of the restoration of the returned remnant of Israel from exile in Babylon. It also marks the beginning of Daniel's "seventy weeks" (Daniel 9:20-27) and provides historical background for the book of Malachi. Much of the material in the book comes from what must have been Nehemiah's personal diary, so frank and vivid is the reporting.[15]

There you are! Thank the Spirit for leading you. He's a wonderful Teacher. Ask for His help as you dig deeper the rest of this week.

Day 3: Pray for the Holy Spirit to lead you as you search. Review the historical information you compiled yesterday. Let's find out a little more about the person of Nehemiah today.

Study Tip: The first few verses of a book often establish important details. Look for places, dates, names, and greetings at the beginning. Cross-reference each detail or look to the footnotes to determine quick context.

1. Go back to the introduction of Nehemiah and make notes about who he was.
2. Look in your topical index (usually in the back of your Bible) under *Nehemiah* and find key verses that describe him.
3. Read Nehemiah 1:1-2. Cross-reference or read the footnotes for the following information:
   - "the month Chislev" (NASB) or "Kislev" (NIV)—see Zechariah 7:1
   - "in the twentieth year"—see Nehemiah 2:1
   - "I was in Susa the capitol" (NASB) or "the citadel of Susa" (NIV)—see Esther 1:2; Daniel 8:1-2
   - "Hanani, one of my brothers"—see Nehemiah 7:2
4. Flip through Nehemiah and look for any other helps (charts, lists, inset information, maps) that offer additional information on him specifically.
5. If you have one, use a Bible handbook for further discovery. Or do what I do and check out www.bible-history.com. Click on *search* and type in *Nehemiah* if you didn't yesterday.
6. Review your notes. Ask the Holy Spirit to help you process the information. Take a closer look. Can you draw any conclusions about the kind of person Nehemiah was? Can you make any inferences? Consider what you've learned about the condition of his homeland, Israel. What picture is painted of Nehemiah? Process your thoughts in your journal.

Day 4: Thank the Spirit for walking down unfamiliar paths with you. He's with you through every cross-reference and footnote. Don't leave Him out.

Now let's begin reading some of Nehemiah. Keep the context of Israel and the details of Nehemiah's life in constant focus.

1. Read 1:1-11. Write a one- or two-sentence summary of this exchange.

2. Next let's look at the details. The following are questions *I'd* consider while journaling through these verses. Feel free to use any of these prompts as you unfold this passage. Don't use every one. Focus on just a few so your responses can be deeper. This is not a list of questions to "answer." They are offered to facilitate a healthy interaction with Scripture. Use them to teach you how to ask your own questions of Scripture.

   • Verse 3: What troubled the Israelites so much about the destruction of the wall and gates of Jerusalem? Based on the previous 150 years of Israel's history, why were the wall and gates around the capital city so important?

   • Verses 3-4: Why did Nehemiah grieve intensely "for days"?

   • The *NIV Study Bible* references Ezra 4:7-23 in the footnote. Read over that passage and expand your understanding of Nehemiah's grief.

   • Verses 5-11: What do you notice about Nehemiah's prayer? What can you learn from this exchange? Slow down and pay attention. Listen to the Spirit.

   • Can you identify the different themes of his prayer?

- What do you notice about the tone of his prayer? How did he approach and speak to God?
- In verse 9, Nehemiah referred to God's promise. Does your cross-reference identify where God orignally made that promise? Check it out.
- Verse 10: Nehemiah says of Israel, "They are Your servants and Your people," as if he's urging God to remember. Glance again at the background information you compiled. Given their recent history, how would you envision the state of their faith? What would it have been like?

3. What do you need to pray about? How has Nehemiah touched you so far? Let your time in the Word fuel your time in prayer.

Day 5: Don't you love Nehemiah? Isn't he the best? Ask the Spirit to build on the foundation of knowledge you've acquired. Ask to be stretched and be willing to reach farther.

1. Review Nehemiah 1 briefly. Now let's read what "fasting and praying before the God of heaven" got him. Read Nehemiah 2:1-10 without stopping.

2. What do you see immediately? What pops right out at you? Write through it and allow the Spirit to fill your mind.

3. Feel free to use any of the following thoughts—not all of them—as a *starting point*, or allow the Spirit to guide you through the significance of this Scripture on your own. Either way, let Him lead you as only He knows how. He may want to show you something specific that applies to your life today.

- Verse 1: Nehemiah approached King Artaxerxes "in the month Nisan." Does your footnote tell you when that was? The lapse between 1:1 and 2:1 was four months. Any thoughts about what might have happened in that span of time?
- Verse 2: Nehemiah said that he "was very much afraid." In 1:11, he asked for "favor in the presence of this man [Artaxerxes]" (NIV). The cross-reference listed yesterday for 1:4 was Ezra 4:7-24. Read that passage if you haven't already. Does this intensify Nehemiah's task in your mind? How do you think he felt coming before the king, given this piece of history?
- Verse 4: What can you learn from Nehemiah in this verse?
- Verse 5: Wow! This is the first we hear of Nehemiah's plan of action. What are your thoughts about this? Could he have chosen to get involved on a lesser scale? (Ask yourself, *What would I have been willing to do?*)
- Verses 5,7-8: Do you see any similarity between the ways Nehemiah spoke to his heavenly King (see 1:5-11) and his earthly king? What was Nehemiah like? How would you characterize him so far?
- Verse 8: Whoa. He hasn't even left Persia yet. What does this verse tell you about his abilities as a visionary?
- End of verse 8: Nehemiah gives us a sidebar in his journal. What does this statement say to you? Consider this in conjunction with his boldness.

Day 6: Pray for strong leadership from the Holy Spirit today. Ask Him to show you truth very clearly.

One more day with Nehemiah. I hope you're intrigued enough to finish studying this book on your own. (I don't want to ruin the ending, but he rebuilds the walls in only fifty-two days. I'm just saying it's a good story.)

1. Let's go on. Read Nehemiah 2:11-20 without stopping. Then go back for a closer look.

Study Tip: If you ever get stuck, one of the quickest ways to deepen insight in the study of a person is to put yourself in his or her shoes. How would you have felt? What would you have done? How would you have responded? Identifying with the character and his or her circumstances instantly gives you perspective.

2. What does the Spirit lead you to initially? In your journal, process through what He is showing you. Ask questions. Pay closer attention. What do you see?

   Here are some additional thoughts to consider. Reflect on any that interest you or use them as a springboard for something different. Let these types of questions be examples to you as you learn to ask them on your own. They are simply an inspection of the details.

   • Verses 12,16: What can you infer from these verses? What does Nehemiah's silence tell you about his leadership? What can you learn from his example?

   • Verses 13-15: If you haven't already, look for a

map or diagram of this beaten-down Jerusalem or the rebuilt city in your study Bible. Check out the dimensions and scope of this project. Does this type of extreme engineering and labor seem plausible for a scholarly cupbearer accustomed to the comforts and privileges of the palace?

- Verses 17-18: Read how Nehemiah led these leaders. What opposition might he have faced in this circle? How did he lead these men? What strategies did he use? How did they respond? Can you apply any of this to leadership responsibilities in your life?
- Verses 19-20: Sanballat the Horonite, Tobiah the Ammonite official, and Geshem the Arab opposed Nehemiah (see also verse 10). What can you discover about them from cross-references or footnotes? Why were they so adamantly against Nehemiah's vision?
- Don't you love verse 20? What can you learn about conflict and confrontation from Nehemiah's example?
- Moment of unity: The cross-reference listed for verse 20 is Acts 8:18-23. Read up on (my favorite) Peter, paying special attention to verse 21. What is God consistently telling us in His Word?

Close this week in prayer, thanking the Spirit for all He has taught you so far and asking for what you still need from Him in the Word.

Week 5

Again, if you have only five days, you may combine Days 1 and 2.

Day 1: Are you encountering the Word in a fresh way? Pray for special guidance this final week as we press toward intimacy.

Read chapter 8, "It's All About Me," and the afterword.

Day 2: Ask the Holy Spirit to personalize His Word to you today. Read it as your own.

Allow your heart to dwell where your mind has gone. We're going to do some work in one of my favorite books, Ephesians.

1. Turn to Ephesians 2:1-10. Read straight through and establish the main idea with a title or sentence.

2. Refer to the suggested questions for personal connection in chapter 8—or find them under "Journaling Strategies" on pages 149–154. There is much richness in these ten verses. Did a word, phrase, or idea jump out at you? Ask the Holy Spirit to lead you through the passage again and explore your response in your journal. Take it straight to heart. This isn't just about the world or other people—it's about you.

Study Tip: Look for transitional phrases in Scripture that connect two parts or establish an order or cause/effect, such as "for this reason," "so that," "so then," "therefore," or "in order to." We usually read over these, but they frequently establish context.

Here are some other thought starters. Look them over and allow them to broaden your perspective. Can you see different ways to interact with Scripture? It's not always simply asking, "What does this mean? What does that mean?" Use *one or two* of the following and allow the Spirit to carry you as you write. Don't allow the quick "answer" to be your goal. Learn to process through Scripture. Where you begin in your journal may not be where you end up. My goal is not to teach you the answers but the *questions*.

- Can you identify progressive steps in this passage? What is God doing in and through us?
- Verses 2-3, NIV: "When you followed the ways of this world." How does this relate to your history?
  - What ways condoned by this world have seduced you?
  - Verse 3: "Indulging the desires of the *flesh* and of the *mind*." What sinful desires are you tempted to indulge?
- Verses 4-5 contain the hope of the world. The very essence of God and His salvation are summed up here.
  - Have you taken this for granted in your life? Do you need to confess apathy toward the grace that brought you to life even as you were dead in your sin?
  - Do you know anything about the author, Paul? If you do, how special is it that he wrote these words? He knew a little something about this, didn't he?
- Verse 6: What does it mean that "God raised us up

with Christ and seated us with him in the heavenly realms in Christ Jesus" (NIV)?

- This type of Bible wording often gets read over quickly. Slow down, cross-reference, and spend time with the significance of this verse. What is the Spirit showing *you* about it?

- Verse 7 begins "in order that" or "so that," which indicates that the first six verses exist for the purpose of what Paul tells us in this verse. What are your insights on this?

- Verses 8-9: How do you feel about grace? Do you accept it? Live in it? Try to earn it?
  - What is so hard about living in grace?
  - Do you have any works that you tend to place pride in?

- Verse 10: One of my favorites! You are His workmanship! His handiwork! He is so proud of you! What good works has God prepared for you to accomplish? What is your calling? What is your passion? What were you made to do for Him?

Read through your response and offer your insights, your questions, your praise, and your heart back to God through prayer.

Day 3: Yesterday you read about the beauty of being saved by grace. Today we get to celebrate being united as believers under that grace. Spend time with the Spirit. He should be your Friend by now.

1. Read Ephesians 2:11-22 without stopping. This would be a great passage to read in a modern translation such

as the *New Living Translation* or the *Contemporary English Version*. Jot down the theme and reread the passage.

2. Let's personalize Scripture today. Go through this passage and rewrite all or parts of it, inserting your name, "I," or "me" when appropriate (example: "I used to be separate from Christ"). You can expand on a sentence if you'd like. Read it out loud when you're done (seriously) and spend time in prayer—not asking for things or praying for others but thanking God for adopting you. He didn't have to, but He loved you into grace. You'll never be a stranger again.

Day 4: Pray for the Spirit to hold you tight in His Word today. Feel His presence. He's there.

1. Turn to Ephesians 3:14-21 and read straight through. This passage is so good, I almost can't stand it.

2. What do you need to write about? How is the Spirit pressing you? What section touched a nerve? Personally respond to these verses. Give Him time to stretch you as you write.

3. Today, write this passage in whole or in part back to God *as a prayer* (example: "I want You to root me in love until I'm grounded, God, because I get uprooted so easily right now"). Adapt the wording however you need to. Expand a sentence if you desire. Add additional comments to a verse if it suits your heart. Pray it to Him in writing. If a verse expresses a concept that isn't true for you now but you want it to be, write it as a request. Be honest in your prayer. This

isn't supposed to be beautifully worded so you can show it off to your small group. It's supposed to be real. Write it out to God and then pray it out loud to Him.

Day 5: Don't you love God's Word? Do you hear how much He loves you? Pray for a growing, healthy relationship with God's Word. This is just the beginning.

1. Read Ephesians 4:1-6. Notice that it begins with "therefore," which tells you that everything you discovered so far points to what Paul writes in this next section. In other words, because God lavished you with undeserved grace, because you as a Gentile now have access to faith, because God dwells in you, because He loves you with a depth you'll never understand, and because He can do more in you than you could ever even dream, *therefore* . . .

2. Take this momentum and write your insights in your journal. Go. If you get stuck, remember that you have many options at your fingertips from which to *choose* (look up the original meaning, read a different translation, use a dictionary or thesaurus, cross-reference, check out the footnotes, ask "why" of something, relate this passage to Paul, relate this passage to the people of Ephesus, rewrite it, journal it as a prayer, connect it to a personal experience, *or* simply allow the Spirit to lead you uniquely).

3. What has He shown you? What is He trying to teach you? Thank the Spirit for loving you and leading you as an individual. He is completely focused on you.

Day 6: Well, here we are. I pass you off to the capable hands of the Spirit. My entire goal is to leave you more confident in the Word, connected to your Helper, and growing in knowledge. You're working out that salvation as God told you to.

Flip back through your journal and take a look at where the Spirit has carried you. Spiritual maturity is a journey, but you've taken some large, substantial steps down that path.

1. Spend some time today in your journal doing the following:
   - Thanking the Spirit for what has impacted you most
   - Praising Him for your favorite insights
   - Asking for help where you still need it
   - Committing to a specific time every day when you'll meet with Him in the Word

2. Close with Psalm 119:11-16. Write it in your journal as your prayer of thanksgiving, adoration, insight, and commitment.

* * * Leader's Guide * * *

This guide is designed to lead a small group through this book in five weeks and then launch immediately into a study of a book of the Bible, implementing the new strategies discussed. I've included optional reading schedules for a few of the smaller books that would extend the total time frame to nine to eleven weeks. The reading schedule should be handed out at the end of the first five weeks.

Each woman will need:

- A copy of this book
- A lined journal

Consider including one of these study tools in the total cost to further equip your girls:

- Bible handbook (see suggestions on page 120)
- Alternate translation in paperback, such as *The Message* or the *New Living Translation*

Small-group discussion will take between sixty and ninety minutes. Feel free to add to that time with worship, activities, or a large-group session.

This material is best conveyed through healthy discussion.

The perfect small-group leader for this study does not have to be a teacher but rather a gifted *facilitator* with a passion for God's Word. The Holy Spirit is the featured Teacher in this study, so leaders need to allow His work to take center stage. The ideal size for a group is eight to twelve women. I highly suggest leaders stay at least two weeks ahead in this study so they can offer advance guidance if necessary.

Each week in the leader's guide is based on the *completion* of that same week in the study guide. The week *before* Week 1 will be your first official meeting day to hand out materials, divide into small groups, and discuss the time frame. Give women an idea of the time they'll need to invest each week for five weeks. Tell them they should plan on half an hour a day, five or six days a week. If they can't imagine spending this much time, ask them to try just reading the book chapters during Week 1 and praying about whether they can deal with this commitment.

Week 1 (Discussion after the first week of study is completed)

As the leader, set the example by having your Bible and journal open and ready every week. Establish the beginning of each session with prayer. Ask for discernment and courage.

Refer to Days 1 through 4 in the study guide. Use the questions from each day for group discussion. You don't necessarily have to hit every single point and subpoint, but lead your group through the primary considerations. Create an atmosphere of authenticity by voicing your own insecurities and struggles in the Word, past or present. Be sure to ask *every* woman what time and place she chose to meet with God daily. Encourage everyone to share.

Keep the discussion to an average of fifteen minutes for each day of study.

Have your girls open to their journal for Day 5. Using their first list of phrases from Psalm 119 (their feelings about the Word), facilitate a prayer time voicing these Scriptures back to God one phrase at a time:

Your word I have treasured in my heart. (verse 11)

Your testimonies also are my delight;
They are my counselors. (verse 24)

Don't embellish or add commentary. Simply pray God's Word. You begin with a phrase and then allow your girls to randomly pray out loud. When you think they've had enough time, transition to the second list of phrases (asking for God's help in the Word) and pray those back to Him in the same way:

Open my eyes, that I may behold
Wonderful things from Your law. (verse 18)

Make me understand the way of Your precepts. (verse 27)

Lead by example. Even those most timid about praying in public can feel safe voicing one line of Scripture out loud. Close when your girls are done.

Before you break, remind them that next week requires six days of study instead of five. If they need to, they may combine Days 1 and 2.

The remaining four weeks of small-group material will be primarily a discussion through Scripture rather than through the content of this book. The focus is on the *application* of study strategies rather than the strategies themselves. Our goal is to foster independence in the Word for every woman by encouraging her to immediately put into practice what she's learned. The learning curve is sped up as women learn from each other in discussion—both in scriptural content and study methods.

Week 2

Open with prayer, asking the Holy Spirit to lead discussion. Ask Him to teach the group through what He revealed individually this week.

Briefly discuss chapter 5 (ten minutes max).

- What strategies did you learn?
- What stood out to you?
- Was anything confusing? Do you have any questions?

Refer to Days 1 through 5 in the study guide. Facilitate discussion using the questions from each day. This time is about what God showed each woman in the Word as she employed new strategies. Spend an average of fifteen minutes on each day of study.

Close with sentence-praying. Women can voice *one or two* simple sentences randomly. They can pray a thanksgiving, a request, a praise, a need, anything. These are the goals:

- To encourage women to become bolder in Bible study and prayer in a nonthreatening manner
- To discourage long, wordy, "religious" prayers that thrive on phraseology and waste valuable time (see Matthew 6:7-8)

Explain the format of the prayer and then model for them by beginning with *one* simple sentence such as, "You are awesome in Your Word, God."

Let your girls off the hook a bit by reminding them that next week has five days of study rather than six.

Week 3

Begin with prayer. Invite the Spirit to stretch the boundaries of your group.

Facilitate a short discussion on chapter 6 (ten minutes or so).

- What do you think about these study tools?
- Did you assemble any new ones?
- What was your favorite tool? Your most challenging tool?
- Did you organize your study space? (Hold your girls accountable!)

Refer to Days 2 through 5 in the study guide. Guide discussion through each day spent in Scripture, using the prompts and questions. The goal is to have women sharing what the Spirit taught them. The tools are simply the means to that end. Move discussion along so that all five days get discussed (about fifteen minutes per day).

End with guided prayer. Have your girls bow their heads and then lead them through these Scripture prompts. Give them two to three minutes after each prompt to pray silently. They are from Daniel 2:20-23 (NIV):

- Say, "Daniel 2:20 — 'Praise be to the name of God forever and ever; wisdom and power are his.' Spend

a couple of minutes praising God not just for what
He does but for who He is. Give Him the honor He
deserves."

- Then say, "Daniel 2:21 — 'He changes times and
seasons; he sets up kings and deposes them. He gives
wisdom to the wise and knowledge to the discerning.' Thank God for the season you are in, even if it's
stormy. Ask Him what He wants to teach you in this
season. Pray to become His discerning daughter who
sees truth clearly."

- Close by saying, "Daniel 2:22-23 — 'He reveals deep
and hidden things; he knows what lies in darkness,
and light dwells with him. I thank and praise you, O
God of my fathers: You have given me wisdom and
power, you have made known to me what we asked
of you.' Thank God for what He revealed to you
this week in His Word. Be specific. Boldly ask Him
to increase your wisdom. Ask Him to show you the
hidden things."

Finally, remind them that Weeks 4 and 5 are designed
to be covered in six days each because they are intensive.
However, women who have only five days may combine
Days 1 and 2.

Week 4

Open with a short prayer giving glory to the Spirit for the
insights shown to your group this week. Ask Him to teach
you during discussion today.

Lead a short discussion on chapter 7 (about ten minutes).

- What were your thoughts on digging into history?
- Where did you find your information?
- Did your study Bible help?

Open your study guide to Days 2 through 6. Work through each day in order, asking the girls to share their findings (allow fifteen minutes per day). Have them include where and how they found their information. For Days 4 through 6, you don't need to ask every question listed, as they were simply suggestions, but let the women share how the Spirit led them. If they answered a question listed, they can mention that in the discussion. We want to move *away* from "answering" a group of questions and *toward* the leadership of the Holy Spirit.

Close with partner-praying. Have the women pair up. Ask them to share authentically about these things:

- The state of their spiritual life
- The health of their marriage (if applicable) or another significant relationship
- Their most pressing need

Have them take turns praying over each other, specifically voicing these needs.

Week 5

Begin with prayer. Ask God to multiply all you've learned. Ask for increased discernment for each woman.

Work progressively through the first five days of study. Allow the women to feed off each other's insights. Keep discussion moving to accomplish all five days (allow fifteen minutes per day). There were fewer prompts this week, so encourage every response that came straight from the Holy Spirit.

Close with Day 6. Ask the women to share their final thoughts and evaluations of their journey.

Lead them through a group prayer. Tell them you will begin a sentence and they can voice a word or short phrase to complete it. Allow several declarations for each starter, such as, "God, You are *compassionate*"; "God, You are *my Teacher*").

- "God, You are . . ."
- "Your Word is . . ."
- "Holy Spirit, You are . . ."
- "You have shown me . . ."
- "Your insights are . . ."
- "Lord, strengthen my . . ."
- "I will meet You in the Word . . ."
- "Spirit, teach me . . ."
- "Thank You for . . ."

Close in thanksgiving for your special group and this journey you've shared.

If your small group will continue meeting, hand out the reading schedule for the book of the Bible you will be studying. Encourage your girls to put into practice all they've learned, rotate through strategies rather than always using the same ones, and be ready to share the first week of independent journaling next week.

Optional Reading Schedules

JAMES

Week 1
1. Research James, his purpose, and his audience
2. James 1:1-4
3. James 1:5-12
4. James 1:13-18
5. James 1:19-27

Week 2
1. James 2:1-7
2. James 2:8-13
3. James 2:14-17
4. James 2:18-20
5. James 2:21-26

Week 3
1. James 3:1-5
2. James 3:6-8
3. James 3:9-12
4. James 3:13-15
5. James 3:16-18

Week 4
1. James 4:1-3
2. James 4:4-6
3. James 4:7-10
4. James 4:11-12
5. James 4:13-17

Week 5
1. James 5:1-4
2. James 5:5-8
3. James 5:9-12
4. James 5:13-16
5. James 5:17-20

1 AND 2 PETER

Week 1

1. Research Peter, his purpose, and his audience
2. 1 Peter 1:1-9
3. 1 Peter 1:10-16
4. 1 Peter 1:17-25
5. 1 Peter 2:1-5

Week 2

1. 1 Peter 2:6-10
2. 1 Peter 2:11-17
3. 1 Peter 2:18-25
4. 1 Peter 3:1-4
5. 1 Peter 3:5-7

Week 3

1. 1 Peter 3:8-12
2. 1 Peter 3:13-17
3. 1 Peter 3:18-22
4. 1 Peter 4:1-6
5. 1 Peter 4:7-11

Week 4

1. 1 Peter 4:12-19
2. 1 Peter 5:1-7
3. 1 Peter 5:8-11
4. 1 Peter 5:12–2 Peter 1:3
5. 2 Peter 1:4-7

Week 5

1. 2 Peter 1:8-11
2. 2 Peter 1:12-18
3. 2 Peter 1:19–2:3
4. 2 Peter 2:4-11
5. 2 Peter 2:12-16

Week 6

1. 2 Peter 2:17-22
2. 2 Peter 3:1-7
3. 2 Peter 3:8-9
4. 2 Peter 3:10-13
5. 2 Peter 3:14-18

RUTH

Week 1

1. Research relevant history
2. Ruth 1:1-5
3. Ruth 1:6-14
4. Ruth 1:15-18
5. Ruth 1:19-22

Week 2

1. Ruth 2:1-3
2. Ruth 2:4-7
3. Ruth 2:8-13
4. Ruth 2:14-17
5. Ruth 2:18-23

Week 3

1. Ruth 3:1-5
2. Ruth 3:6-9
3. Ruth 3:10-14
4. Ruth 3:15-18
5. Ruth 4:1-5

Week 4

1. Ruth 4:6-10
2. Ruth 4:11-12
3. Ruth 4:13-17
4. Ruth 4:18-22

Notes

* * *   * * *

CHAPTER THREE: CODEPENDENCY THAT DOESN'T REQUIRE THERAPY

1. *Ryrie Study Bible*, expanded ed., *New American Standard Version*, Red Letter (Chicago: Moody, 1995), 1709.

CHAPTER SIX: TWEEZERS, VELCRO ROLLERS, AND OTHER TOOLS FOR GIRLS

1. *Ryrie Study Bible*, expanded ed., *New American Standard Version*, Red Letter (Chicago: Moody, 1995), 1790.
2. Taken from "Bible Translations," *Zondervan*, http://www.zondervanbibles.com/translations.htm.
3. Rob Lacey, *The Word on the Street* (Grand Rapids, MI: Zondervan, 2003), back cover.
4. *Roget's New Millennium Thesaurus*, 1st ed., s.v. "guard," http://thesaurus.reference.com/search?q=guard.

CHAPTER SEVEN: IT'S NOT JUST FOR NERDS

1. *Ryrie Study Bible*, expanded ed., *New American Standard Version*, Red Letter (Chicago: Moody, 1995), 422, 1815.

STUDY GUIDE

1. *NIV Study Bible* (Grand Rapids, MI: Zondervan, 2002), 1727.
2. *Ryrie Study Bible*, expanded ed., *New American Standard Version*, Red Letter (Chicago: Moody, 1995), 1809.
3. *Life Application Study Bible, New International Version* (Grand Rapids, MI: Zondervan, 1988), 2051.

4. *The American Heritage Dictionary of the American Language*, 4th ed., s.v. "defend," http://dictionary.reference.com/search?q=defender.

5. *WordNet 2.0*, s.v. "rebellious," (Princeton, NJ: Princeton University, 2003), http://dictionary.reference.com/search?q=rebellious.

6. *The American Heritage Dictionary of the American Language*, 4th ed., s.v. "rebellious," http://dictionary.reference.com/search?q=rebellious.

7. *The American Heritage Dictionary of the American Language*, 4th ed., s.v. "rebel," http://dictionary.reference.com/search?q=rebel.

8. *The American Heritage Dictionary of the American Language*, 4th ed., s.v. "refreshed," http://dictionary.reference.com/search?q=refreshed.

9. *The American Heritage Dictionary of the American Language*, 4th ed., s.v. "settled," http://dictionary.reference.com/search?q=settled.

10. *Roget's New Millennium Thesaurus*, 1st ed., s.v. "fatherless," http://thesaurus.reference.com/search?q=fatherless.

11. *Roget's New Millennium Thesaurus*, 1st ed., s.v. "lonely," http://thesaurus.reference.com/search?q=lonely.

12. *Roget's New Millennium Thesaurus*, 1st ed., s.v. "parched," http://thesaurus.reference.com/search?q=parched.

13. *Roget's New Millennium Thesaurus*, 1st ed., s.v. "before," http://thesaurus.reference.com/search?q=before.

14. *Roget's New Millennium Thesaurus*, 1st ed., s.v. "inheritance," http://thesaurus.reference.com/search?q=inheritance.

15. *Ryrie Study Bible*, 722, 738.

About The Author

* * * * *

Jen has partnered with her husband, Brandon, in full-time ministry for nine years while keeping her vow never to wear suntan pantyhose and white flats. If you catch her in either of those, please contact her girlfriends immediately so they can stage an intervention. Although she has purchased either a new outfit or new shoes every single time she's been invited as a speaker, she is still happily married after eleven years (to the same man). Jen lives in beautiful Austin, Texas, but has somehow avoided becoming a runner, a bicyclist, a granola, or an earth-conscious recycler.

Jen intensely loves God, Jesus, her church, Scripture, writing, teaching, women, and finding the funny and profound in all these things. She surrounds herself with friends who, if not technically insane, are at least reassuringly dysfunctional. If nothing else, their lives provide amusing anecdotes should her own family ever become normal. However, her three kids—Gavin, Sydney Beth, and Caleb—have definitively squashed any notion that her life will ever be normal (see all stories included in this book). She recently crossed the threshold into her thirties, feigning indifference, where she now happily resides as a pretend grown-up. This book, her first, is irrefutable evidence that God can use *anyone* to do His work.

For more information on Jen's ministry or to schedule her for your conference, retreat, or speaking engagement, go to www.jenhatmaker.com. You can also write to her at 7509 Callbram Lane, Austin, Texas, 78736.

Empower your girlfriends with a smart new way to study the Bible.

Road Trip
Jen Hatmaker
978-1-57683-892-1

Road trips are as much about the journey as they are their ultimate destinations, and who better to travel with than your best Girlfriends? You navigate life together, why not the Bible? Guided by Abram, the Samaritan woman, Peter, Paul, and Jesus Himself, you're guaranteed the trip of a lifetime!

Tune In
Jen Hatmaker
978-1-57683-893-8

God has given us the tools and written them down for us to read and study, but have we learned how to really tune in to them? You may think you've got a one-sided relationship with God, but He's in constant dialogue with you. Are you ready to tune Him in?